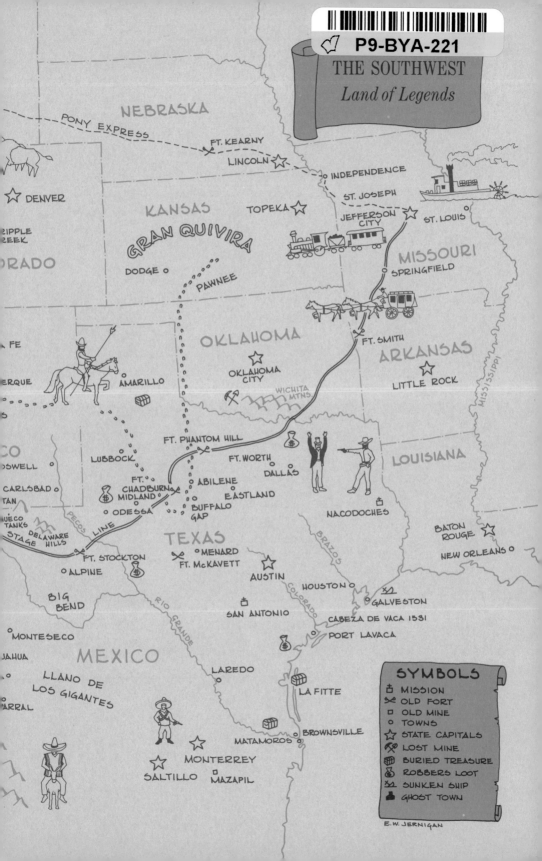

Fantasies of Gold

LEGENDS OF TREASURES
AND HOW THEY GREW

Fantasies of Gold

E. B. "TED" SAYLES

with JOAN ASHBY HENLEY

THE UNIVERSITY OF ARIZONA PRESS
TUCSON, ARIZONA

About the Authors . . .

E. B. SAYLES, curator of the Arizona State Museum from 1943 until his retirement in 1961, turned professional archaeologist in 1931 when he adopted Arizona as his home state. A native Texan, he is co-founder of the Texas Archaeological Society. His list of professional memberships includes also the Society for American Archaeology, American Anthropological Society, Arizona Academy of Science, Sigma Xi, and the Arizona Archaeological and Historical Society. His scientific and popular publications are on topics from Southwestern archaeology as well as the crafts and arts of Indians and of Mexico, and he is author of a series of juvenile books on the history of pre-Columbian America.

JOAN ASHBY HENLEY is a free-lance author who has placed special emphasis on her feature writing about the Southwest areas with which she was personally familiar. She is a granddaughter of Nogales, Arizona, territorial pioneers and formerly was a staff writer for the *Nogales Daily Herald*.

THE UNIVERSITY OF ARIZONA PRESS

Contents

ILLUSTRATIONS

THE AUTHOR AND ONE OF HIS BEST FRIENDS on a jaunt that became a journey of more than forty years and 80,000 miles searching for prehistoric sites in the Southwest and excavating some to learn what they might tell.

But the search uncovered more than archaeology alone — it uncovered fantasies and visions of buried treasure and lost mines as well.

What's This All About?

THIS IS AN ACCOUNT of what I learned of how Southwestern legends of treasure may have come about from visions — something that is seen only in one's mind (call it by any other term). When a vision is so real that it is believed actually to have taken place then a legend is born.

Legendary treasures are those that exist only in one's mind, and they do not include SALVAGE (the recovery of losses based on documents, such as shipwrecks); ARCHAEOLOGY (remains of the past) though legends may be created about them; and JUNK (bottles, metal and other scrap) frequently described in stories telling of the search for legendary precious metals.

In spite of persistent rumor, nothing that represents wealth as we know it has ever been found in the archaeological ruins north of Mexico. Their inhabitants had not learned the use of metal except for small objects of copper, which had been made in Mexico, like the bell given Cabeza de Vaca in his journey across Texas. At most, archaeological wealth in the Southwest is represented by ornaments made of shell, stone (some turquoise), wood, seed, and bone. Other artifacts — pottery, stone and bone tools, and wooden objects — are of more concern to the archaeologist and to the collector than to the treasure hunter.

I have never known of a *legendary* treasure (one that exists in one's mind) that has ever been found — unless one considers that the real wealth in America discovered by Spanish explorers was in fulfillment of the dreams of mankind since early times. But I am sure this account will not stop the dyed-in-the-wool treasure hunter from looking. I will be surprised if it does not start some searching for the legendary treasures I encountered.

My conclusions about legendary treasures have been fashioned of the accounts of those who have known of buried treasures and lost mines; of my own knowledge of some of the places where treasures are sought and, especially, of some of the peculiar things that provide the clues to their hidden places around which legends have grown.

I first began to learn about them in the early 1920's when I became interested in the archaeology of the Southwest. Much of the country was then sparsely settled, as some of it still is, with many large tracts of land in ranches, forests, Indian reservations, and other public holdings. The Southwest was then unspoiled by the "progress" that had left its mark

1

on the rest of the country — the crowding of people in sprawling centers of population; the despoiling of the land for uses the arid country repelled; and the increase in crime. Texas was a friendly region, its reputation carried over from the name of the Indians found there by the Spanish explorers — the Tejas.

When I started looking for archaeological sites in Texas in the 1920's, the people who lived in isolated places were eager to talk to a stranger such as I. But it seemed odd to many of them, I am sure, that I should be looking for old Indian ruins. Some were convinced that I was really looking for buried treasure. Why should archaeologists confine themselves only to old relics?

During the years that followed, I learned that many of those whom I asked about archaeological sites had read or heard about the riches that had come from past civilizations. Some of these riches could be seen in many museums. Some of the greatest and most publicized treasures were those from Egyptian tombs — the tomb of King Tutankhamen, in particular. There were American treasures that the Spanish and later looters overlooked: Tomb 7, at Monte Albán, Oaxaca, Mexico; the gold objects still being recovered from the Sacred Well (cenote) at Chichén Itzá in Yucatan; and objects from the burials found in the coastal deserts of South America. Wrecked ships, carrying rich cargoes, had been salvaged. People also knew of the early mines in the Southwest that were first worked from the rich surface deposits like those in Nevada, which produced millions of dollars' worth of silver, as well as the gold strikes in California and Alaska. And especially of the rich Mexican mines.

These riches were all real. Why should archaeologists spend their time looking for broken pieces of pottery at old ruins when there was so much treasure to seek?

When I asked about archaeological remains I sometimes heard of legendary lost treasures. Some landowners refused permission to go on their property until I assured them that I was not looking for anything but Indian ruins, and that if I found anything else I would tell them about it (such arrangements are common practice). These misunderstandings were frustrating but always fascinating.

By listening to the often repeated legends, I sometimes picked up bits of information that led to a cave that had been home to somebody long before Columbus arrived in America. Sometimes a ruin turned out to be an ancient one and not some abandoned ranch house nearly demolished by treasure hunters digging alongside the old walls.

The more I learned about legends the more fascinated I became, not only with the stories themselves but with a curiosity to learn how a Southwestern treasure legend — such as those often told to me and which

I later read about — is started. Why does it become so real to its creator that he not only comes to believe it but convinces others, too.

The different kinds of things often used by treasure hunters as clues in their search for mythical wealth were even more fascinating to me than the legends themselves. Some of these clues were archaeological features, and when I became curator of the Arizona State Museum, I again heard many of the legends that I had been told when I was carrying on field work. Treasure hunters often asked about the clues they thought were significant in their search for legendary wealth. So my curiosity about the origin of Southwestern treasure legends has been kept alive during all my adult life.

It was not until many years had passed and I had heard the legends told by those who sometimes spent their lifetime looking for mythical wealth — myths they had created from certain clues — that I finally began to find some answers.

ACKNOWLEDGMENTS

THIS BOOK could never have been written without the help of hundreds of people throughout the Southwest who gave their time and much information since I first became interested in archaeology.

Many of them were business and professional men who devoted their spare time to locating the old ruins within reach of holiday and weekend trips; some were farmers, ranchers, their wives, and the small boys who always knew the best places to look for arrowheads. Some of them have made collections and records from different parts of the country that have become important to the museums which now possess them

There were also many collectors with different hobbies who knew the surrounding country. Some collections were specialized, but others started at that time have grown into the many roadside "museums" throughout the Southwest which are crammed with curiosities of all sorts. They have become an adjunct to little businesses, some dealing in minerals, others in "antiques" and second-hand things of all sorts, some being eating places, others being filling stations.

Some of these people who gave their time to my search for archaeology were chance acquaintances remembered only as I might have recorded their names in field notes. Many of those I knew in the 1920's are no longer living. But this is my acknowledgment to all.

This is also an acknowledgment to those who shared some of their own experiences with me by telling me of them while I was active as an archaeologist and museum curator: Mr. and Mrs. R. B. Alves, El Paso, Texas; the Brownfield family, Buffalo Gap, Texas; Mr. O. S. Connolly, Bowie, Arizona; Mr. Roscoe P. Conkling, El Paso, Texas; Colonel M. C.

Crimmins, San Antonio, Texas; "Uncle" John Hands, Rodeo, New Mexico; Carl and Ethel Larsen, Walnut Springs, Arizona; Mr. Gus McGinnis, Las Varas, Chihuahua; Mr. George C. Martin, Rockport, Texas; Mr. Floyd V. Studer, Amarillo, Texas; and Mr. Victor J. Smith, Alpine, Texas.

I should also like to thank all the old-time first settlers in West Texas whom I once knew in the town where I was born — Abilene — and who lived through the buffalo-hunting, Indian-fighting, cattle-driving, railroad-building, pioneer days.

Many others have directly helped in writing the book. First, Joan Ashby Henley has collaborated with me in the chore of keeping the story my own and at the same time preventing it from becoming a rambling reminiscence.

The "we" of my personal experiences includes one or more of those who shared most of them with me, not always as enthusiastically, but without complaint: my wife, the late Gladys Cheatham Sayles; Carl Chelf; Johnny Olguin; and Charles Renfroe.

So many have helped in different ways in the writing of the book that I am listing below only those who read the manuscript, or parts of it, and helped in the preparation of the pictures and text: Robert G. Baker, Curator, Arizona State Museum; Thomas W. Bent, San Diego, California; Mrs. Rodney (Kathleen Clonts) Clifford, Tucson; Orville A. Cochran, Director, Fort Huachuca Museum; George Eckhart, Historian, Tucson; Bernard L. Fontana, Ethnologist, Arizona State Museum; Cynthia Colby Gabrielli, Librarian, Cambridge, Massachusetts; Frances Gillmor, Folklorist, University of Arizona; Emil W. Haury, Director Emeritus, Arizona State Museum; Milton R. Hunter, First Council of the Seventy, Church of Jesus Christ of Latter Day Saints, Salt Lake City; Florence Lawson, Executive Secretary, Escondido, California; Fred Linquist, Prescott, Arizona; John Riddick, Science Writer, *Tucson Daily Citizen;* George Roseveare, Mining Engineer, Arizona Bureau of Mines; Watson Smith, Director, Peabody Museum of Archaeology, West of the Pecos River, Tucson; and Raymond H. Thompson, Head, Department of Anthropology, Director Arizona State Museum, University of Arizona.

Many inquiries were made about the Elephant Slabs. They have generally aroused speculation and puzzlement, and I am indebted to the following for their response: J. O. Brew, Director, Peabody Museum, Harvard University, Cambridge, Massachusetts; H. Thomas Cain, Director, Heard Museum, Phoenix, Arizona; Ross T. Christensen, Anthropologist, Brigham Young University, Provo, Utah; Alfred E. Dittert, Archaeologist, Museum of New Mexico, Santa Fe, New Mexico; Frank E. Eddy, Archaeologist, Museum of New Mexico, Santa Fe, New Mexico;

Gordon F. Ekholm, Anthropologist, American Museum of Natural History, New York; I. F. Flora, Archaeologist, Durango, Colorado; White Bear (Oswald Fredericks), Hopi Artist, Sedona, Arizona; Harold S. Gladwin, Former Director, Gila Pueblo, Santa Barbara, California; Charles O. Houston, Research Consultant, University of Manila, Manila; Jesse D. Jennings, Anthropologist, University of Utah, Salt Lake City, Utah; Aileen O'Bryan, Folklorist, Santa Fe, New Mexico; Deric O'Bryan, Anthropologist, Washington, D.C.; Roland Richert, Archaeologist, National Park Service; Donald Scott, Director Emeritus, Peabody Museum, Harvard University, Cambridge, Massachusetts; Don Watson, Archaeologist, Cortez, Colorado; Jack R. Williams, Superintendent, Aztec Ruins National Monument; Richard B. Woodbury, Anthropologist, National Museum, Washington, D.C.; and Barton A. Wright, Curator, Museum of Northern Arizona, Flagstaff, Arizona.

All photographs were made by the author, with the exception of those credited to other sources which include the late Henry Sayles, Jr.; the Post Signal Photographic Laboratory, U.S. Army Electronic Proving Grounds, Fort Huachuca, Arizona; John Riddick, *Tucson Daily Citizen;* Clifton Abbott, Tucson; the University of Oklahoma Library, Rose Collection; and the Arizona State Museum.

E. B. "TED" SAYLES

BY CANOE on the Colorado River of Texas en route to the University at Austin, in the summer of 1913.

This was my first introduction to the archaeology of Texas — other than picking up arrowheads then found "everywhere." The "burnt-rock mounds," large accumulations of earth stones, were common along every stream in central Texas. Sometimes the fire-cracked rocks from the old campfires covered acres. There the prehistoric people had lived mainly on fresh-water mussels, cactus, fruits, and the thick trunks of yucca (agave-mescal) plants, which were roasted in earthen pits.

Two of us made the two-month trip for a total of $35.40. Butter cost ten cents a pound; two chickens and a dozen eggs, seventy-five cents. Fish, squirrels, and rabbits, supplemented by wild grapes and fruits, kept us well fed.

The summer rains far to the west dumped their floods into the river, and we rode the swell, ahead of the foaming crest, along with the turtles and snakes that crawled onto the logs picked up by the rising water. When the debris — driftwood, unmanned boats, floating outhouses and chicken coops — became too thick, we camped on the bank until the flood passed.

BY HACK on a hunting trip west of the Pecos River in 1920 that turned into a search for Indian trails, marked by piles of stones left in the passes that led through the Delaware Hills, south of the Guadalupe Mountains.

Legends tell of the treasures left by the Indians in the rock piles serving as trail markers, and of places where the arrangements of certain stones and twigs carried messages.

How I Got There

ONCE I FIGURED that I had traveled three times the distance around the world — on foot, on horseback, by wagon, automobile, and plane, looking for archaeological sites in the Southwest since I picked up my first stone arrowhead.

My interest in Southwestern archaeology — especially Texas archaeology — was aroused during the armistice of World War I. My division, the 36th, was held in reserve in France while the politicians laid the groundwork for the next chapter — World War II.

While the daily rains in the winter of 1918-19 turned the land into muddy lakes, my regiment rotated with others to maintain the clay roads that led from the railhead at Ervy-le Chatel (Aube). Trucks hauled gravel from the pits on river terraces. Sometimes, before the gravel was spread on the water-logged roads, one could catch a glimpse of the flint-like material used in making the paleolithic tools, such as were displayed in a corner cabinet of the Château de Mortrie where I was billeted, near Savigné-l'-Évêque (Sarthe) The ancient stone tools reminded me of those I had often seen on the flint-covered hills of central Texas. When I was mustered out, I carried on with what had begun earlier as a hobby — the study of Texas history.

At the time, there was little known of the archaeology of Texas, and even less recorded. So I began to learn, as a weekend amateur, visiting all parts of the state during the next ten years, meeting others who were doing the same sort of thing.

Anyone can learn archaeology, theoretically, from books. To know the experience of other archaeologists calls for some first-hand contact. Too often the results of archaeological field work and subsequent discoveries are delayed in publication or are never made public — perhaps buried forever in the files of some museum or university.

In the 1920's there were few Southwestern archaeologists. I learned directly from them by keeping abreast of their work. When I became a field archaeologist in the 1930's, I found that this experience and what I had learned from books, together with my skills in photography and drawing, my knowledge of the country, and my experience in camp life, were all applicable.

In 1932, during the Depression, I became associated with Gila Pueblo, the research center at Globe, Arizona, in its survey of the Southwest. I planned to stay a year, but the association grew into the job as field archaeologist and ended only with World War II, when Gila Pueblo ceased its activities. By that time, the archaeological survey of the South-west had been completed, along with a program of excavation in parts of Texas, New Mexico, Arizona, and Chihuahua.

I then joined the staff of the Arizona State Museum in Tucson as curator and continued to carry on some archaeological field work until my retirement in 1961.

Whatever part I played in furthering the archaeological knowledge of the Southwest is recorded in professional publications — but so much more was "off the record," and this is that story.

BY HORSEBACK from the Hearst Ranch at Las Varas, Chihuahua, which furnished pack mules and saddle horses for a trip into the barranca country of the Sierra Madre in 1933. Gus McGinnis, the foreman, sent his son along as guide to the cliff dwellings hidden in the deep canyons. Mr. McGinnis and his son provided us with vivid accounts of the legends of buried treasures and lost mines in the vicinity — so vividly, in fact, that we felt we hardly needed luck to find them, only a shovel to dig for them.

BY WAGON with a four-mule team needed to haul our camping gear into the foothills of the Guadalupe Mountains on the New Mexico-Texas line northeast of El Paso. A lost gold mine is said to be somewhere in the canyons that cut deep into the rugged mountains. But our interest was in digging for archaeological remains in the caves.

My wife and friends had come to join us at the nearby tourist cabins where we met Rex, a German police dog. His job was to look after the camp, and he was introduced to each guest by the owner of the ranch on which the little wooden shacks had been built.

While my wife and her friends were sightseeing, we were hard at work in a spot known at Goat Cave. Here the animals had bedded down during the cold weather to escape the wind and in the hot summer to find shade. Their droppings over the years had filled the low shelter almost to the ceiling.

When we finished our dig, we returned to the tourist cabins with thoughts of a hot shower and clean clothes uppermost in our minds. Rex, who was there alone, had different ideas. We didn't smell like the guests he had met earlier.

While the late shadows made the February chill even colder, we retreated to the corral, where the cattle drank at the water trough. There we bathed and soaped our matted hair, shivering while the slippery soap kept falling into the dirt.

After we had dressed in fresh clothes, rolled up our more fragrant ones, and tied them to a corral post, Rex welcomed us as the guests his master had introduced to him earlier.

BY CAR an overnight camp could be made almost anywhere by pulling off the road — when I started my archaeological work. Now the country is fenced, gates locked; to visit many public lands, now used for parks, people must pay a fee.

The archaeological surveying I did in the Southwest was mainly searching for the places where its earliest inhabitants — the Indians and their ancestors — had lived in camps and villages. In these places I found the burned stones of their cooking fires, their burial places, and often the deep, circular-shaped mortar holes in bedrock where the women had once ground their foods, the grinding holes close together so that the women might gossip while they worked. Often there were stone cliffs with rock paintings in color or pecked into the flat, smooth surfaces, showing the kinds of animals that were hunted and probably something of what the people thought. And, of course, there were the ruins of their villages, long since changed to mounds of earth and rocks.

I made a sample collection of the artifacts — bits of pottery, stone tools — as a part of the archaeological record.

BY PLANE — This plane had been reconditioned for training pilots and mechanics in preparation for World War II. In 1947, it was owned by one of those little outfits that had sprung up all over the country — stunt flying, training, making short chartered flights.

The pilot, Dale Lewis of Globe, had promised to fly me over the Point of Pines country on the San Carlos Apache Indian Reservation. There the Arizona State Museum, with the Department of Anthropology, University of Arizona, had set up a field school in archaeology.

Dale buzzed camp and, after he had landed on a dirt road, we took off. A cloud of dust behind us hid the others in camp — including my wife — who had come out to see us off.

At the time, a forest fire had been burning for a week, twenty miles away. We headed for the black plume of smoke that trailed across the sky. The little plane struggled to keep a few hundred feet above ground level — which was 6,000 feet above the sea — until we came to the fire area. Then it shot up high above the cloud of black smoke that boiled up from the hot, blackened forest. After riding the thermals and taking some pictures of the fire and burned-over area, we glided down to treetop level, looking for ruins sometimes more readily seen from the air.

When we returned to camp, my wife met me with a peculiar look and told me that after I had taken off in the plane, she recognized it as one on which she had helped rebuild the fuselage and the wings as a part of her war stint.

"Until you got back," she confessed, "I wondered how good a job we'd done."

—Post Signal Photographic Laboratory, U.S. Army Electronic Proving Ground, Fort Huachuca, Ariz.

"SERGEANT" ROBERT JONES (right) of Dallas, Texas, watches hopefully as a giant clam-shell crane scoops away the covering of an eighteen-year-old dream — several million dollars in gold bullion which he claimed to have seen in 1941.

Sergeant Jones' Treasure

ON SEPTEMBER 17, 1959, a telephone call came to the Arizona State Museum from the Public Relations Office at Fort Huachuca, sixty miles from Tucson.

"If someone from the museum will be here at 9:30 tomorrow morning, he'll learn something of value — that is, if something expected takes place."

"If what takes place?" I asked, trying to understand the mysterious message.

"Sorry," the voice answered. "This is classified. We can't give out anything by telephone."

I was curious, of course. I had been helping Lt. Col. Webster C. Hatfield (U.S. Army Ret.) set up a museum at the fort. Perhaps he might know something about this odd request.

"I know about it," he admitted when I called, "but it's classified and I can't tell you anything. But the museum will find it worthwhile to send someone."

I was skeptical. Could this be a scheme to involve our museum in some promotional stunt? It seemed most unlikely, and the call to Hatfield ruled out the possibility of a practical joke.

At exactly 9:30 the next morning, Bob Baker, later curator of the museum, and I were at the Information Center at the fort. There we were briefed by the post Inspector General, Colonel Eldridge Bacon.

"We're just on the verge of uncovering a ten-million-dollar treasure," the colonel explained. "A Sergeant Jones claimed he found it in a tunnel in one of these canyons while he was stationed here in 1941," he continued.

Bob and I exchanged looks, while the colonel went on describing a "treasure of bars of metal stacked like cordwood in an underground room into which Sergeant Jones had fallen."

Now we knew. The Army, like a great many others, regarded archaeologists as treasure hunters. We had been invited to witness the recovery of the biggest treasure ever buried in the Southwest!

The colonel cautioned us that everything we heard or saw must be kept secret until the discovery was revealed by the Army. The story has since been printed in numerous newspapers and in *Newsweek, Life,* and *Ebony* magazines.

Here is what I saw and have since learned of Sergeant Jones' Treasure.

Sergeant Jones (Private Robert Jones, a Negro, actually using the term "Sergeant" only for prestige purposes) had gone for a walk with a friend into the nearby mountains while stationed at Fort Huachuca in 1941. Jones claimed that he had fallen into an underground cavity, thirty-two feet deep — with a tunnel leading to a room where he saw metal ingots stacked up like cordwood. The ingots were of a definite shape and size, according to Jones — sixteen inches long, four inches wide, and two inches thick. After Jones was helped out by his companion, they rushed back to report their find to their top sergeant.

The top sergeant discredited the story as just another wild tale of buried treasure, Jones said. Later, Jones and his friend returned to the find and hacked off a piece of one of the bars. Jones chiseled his initials once on a flat rock, which he placed in the hole, and again on a nearby spring house. The two men sold the gold, illegally, to a man Jones described as an assayer in a nearby town. For this chunk of metal he received $890, and he promptly spent it all on a party for his buddies on the post.

None of this has been confirmed. Jones' companion had died. Whoever may have bought the gold would hardly admit it, since gold may be purchased only by federal permit.

After 1941, Jones had lived in Dallas where he had convinced friends of the existence of his treasure. Eighteen years later, after many trials, he managed somehow to convince the Army authorities of it, too, although he did not at the time mention the $890.

He was given permission to dig in January, 1959. At first only hand tools were used, but when little progress was made the Army loaned a bulldozer and operators. Then they struck water at fifteen feet, only half-way to the bottom of the underground room where Jones said his treasure lay. They stopped and filled in the hole.

The Army gave up, but not Jones. He had just begun.

Six months later, he showed up at the post with two friends. This time he told the Army personnel the story of the $890, hoping to use it as a clincher. But it wasn't enough. The Army was through looking for his buried treasure. No more digging.

Jones was persistent. In July, he came up with statements from two men who had been stationed with him at the fort and remembered hearing about the gold. In August, he presented his old top sergeant. Though he didn't remember the story of the treasure, the old sergeant did remember Jones as being trustworthy. If Jones said he had seen the gold, the sergeant believed him and thought the Army should help him dig for it.

Thus, in September, 1959, the Army had once again geared up for the treasure hunt. First it used a well-drilling outfit. After drilling with difficulty past large boulders, the bit suddenly met no resistance for a depth of six feet.

"That," Colonel Bacon informed us, "must have been the underground room. Not as deep as we had expected, but this canyon road has been graded since 1941, so that may account for the difference."

We drove along with our escort. By now, we had passed two military police checking points. Ahead was the third, below a fork in the winding canyon. Here the canyon widened out into a park-like place, shaded by tall trees — cottonwoods, sycamores, and mountain ash. It was choked with Army trucks and passenger cars — even civilian ones.

Farther on we could see the swinging boom of a shovel at work and hear the sound of metal clanging against rocks. As we approached, we saw a bull-dozer, a well-drilling rig, and Army signal trucks, with crowds of uniformed personnel and people in civilian dress. The latter were rumored to be representatives of the United States Treasury Department, on hand to take charge of the treasure when it was uncovered. There were also Army photographers and radio and television technicians.

Standing apart from the others was Jones with his two friends, intently watching each shovelful of black muck that was scooped out of the muddy water, now half-filling a gaping hole sixty feet across. Here was the treasure site. Adjoining this area was a small cement spring house, from which water was piped to the fort.

Up and down the canyon I had noticed small mounds of earth, showing where prospectors had sunk shallow pits to meet assessment requirements necessary to hold mining claims. Not far up another fork of the canyon was a boarded-up tunnel, additional evidence of the abandoned hopes of some prospector.

As the hot September sun passed overhead and cool shadows filled the canyon, Army photographers were exploding flash bulbs; public relations men were recording interviews on tapes for radio and television. Those standing around the gaping crater kept their eyes on the shovel, dipping into the muddy water, slowly getting down to the depth where Jones said he had seen the ingots.

Some spoke of the gold that had been mined in the Huachuca Mountains. Others recalled legendary tales of treasure located in every direction from Fort Huachuca.

The shovel stopped work and the operator jumped down from the cab. He hurried to the pile of black muck he had just dumped, and everyone gathered around him while he examined a handful of fine, cream-colored material.

"What is it?" someone asked. "Gold?"

"No. Looks like the stuff that's found in running water."

"Yeah? What's it called?" another asked.

"Tufa," someone answered. "Must have come from where there's running water."

The shovel resumed its work while Jones continued to repeat, to all who would listen, each detail of the story that was real to him and to some others as well. No one could doubt that he believed that he had seen the gold, and that it would be uncovered as soon as the shovel dug just a little bit deeper.

"I know it's there," he said over and over, watching as each load from the shovel was dropped.

"Hey, Jones," a young man called to him, "what'll you do with it when you get it?"

"What the gov'ment don't keep, will go to do good — for kids and poor folks."

Eventually Bob and I were asked what we thought of the chances of fiinding the treasure. Gold is where you find it, was all we could say. But I thought that if we had been called in before the digging had started, we could have pointed out that archaeologists never dig at the spot where they expect to find anything. We start beyond that point and explore carefully. Big shovels are fine to remove the earth from something to be uncovered — but first that something must be located by careful digging with hand tools.

What followed has been recorded in newspapers and magazines. The Army reluctantly called off the work when the excavation was stopped by solid rock. It had done all it had agreed to do — dig in the spot where Jones said his treasure lay buried at a depth of thirty-two feet. No sign had been found of the underground cavity or the tunnel leading to the treasure-filled room.

I wondered. Was it only something that existed in Jones' mind? Something so real that he not only believed it but had convinced others, too? Even the Army had found itself, if not convinced, at least not unbelieving. After all, the Army had checked his story and had found nothing to show that Jones was not honest or trustworthy, though it had found little or nothing that actually confirmed his story, either.

How, then, could it have come about? Could the story, or any parts of it, have taken place?

Was There a Treasure?

HAD THE ARMY really proved or disproved the existence of the treasure?

It had obviously made every effort to check Jones' story with others — his top sergeant and those who knew him at Fort Huachuca. It had used men and equipment to dig extensively at his direction. But no one, I thought, not even the Army, had really checked to find out whether any *single* part of his story could have actually been a fact, and not a figment of his imagination.

Could there have been any kind of an underground opening at the place where the Army dug for treasure?

The small mounds of rock and earth and the boarded-up tunnel indicate that the canyon had been prospected in the past. Maybe it was just the sight of the old tunnel that gave Jones the idea for the whole story. Anyway, there is plenty of evidence to show that in the past a lot of digging had been done in Huachuca Canyon.

Though the bedrock is granite and the fill of the V-shaped canyon is made up of a conglomerate of boulders and rotted granite, some prospectors might nonetheless sink tunnels and shafts into either the floor or the sides of the canyon. There is a tunnel in the Chiricahua Range in southeastern Arizona, dug entirely by hand with the aid of some dynamite. It was made to develop a lead mine more than sixty years ago by the late "Uncle" John Hands and his brother at Paradise on Cave Creek.

Therefore, if there had been extensive digging by early miners where Jones says he fell into a hole in the ground, it would be easy to believe him even if he had described a room twice as large as he did!

Another possibility might have been an excavation resulting from an attempt to develop the water in the canyon. There might even have been a natural underground opening eroded by the flow of water. The tufa that was brought up by the shovel showed that there was either a spring or another source of water in which the deposit had formed.

A mountain cloudburst could have changed the surface appearance of the valley floor, so that when Jones came along, there was just enough of an opening for him to fall into. When the Army drilled at the spot, there was still some sort of cavity below ground, for the bit fell six feet until it hit solid rock. Whatever it was, it might have caved in while the bulldozer was operating or, more likely, while the shovel was working in the water.

A filled-in tunnel probably would not have been noticed during the excavation. It *could* have been recognized had the excavation been started beyond the area where the well-bit dropped into the cavity and then extended into this region. Provided the water was kept pumped out of the site, observations could then have been made to determine whether or not there had been a tunnel. The Army's shovel might actually have dug into a caved-in or filled-in tunnel; but under the circumstances there would have been no way of knowing this— short of hauling up some heavy gold bars.

So Jones *could* have fallen into some sort of a hole in the ground. His imagination *may* have turned it into a room filled with ingots of gold. A lot of people, including the Army, have taken his word for it. I must admit that, when I talked to him, I had the feeling that he had complete faith in what he was saying.

Could there have been any gold ingots of the sort he described?

Jones was very positive about the dimensions of the ingots — sixteen by four by two inches. He had been a stone mason and his eye had been trained to size things accurately.

Such a size would be odd for bullion bars today. Now they are molded so that they can be easily handled. But there was a time in the Southwest when ingots of more or less the size described by Jones would not have been a rarity.

All the early mines were operated in highly individualistic ways. If the bullion had to be hauled on the back of a pack animal, the metal would have been cast in a clay mold of a convenient size made on the spot. The ingots described by Jones, if gold, would weigh about sixty pounds, depending on their purity. Even a burro could carry two of them, balanced on either side of a pack.

Where could the ingots have come from?

If all the legendary gold and silver hidden in the Southwest were lumped together, it would make quite a respectable-sized mountain. One of the greatest hoards, according to legend, is that of the fabulous mines of Toyopa in northern Mexico. They have been hunted since 1530, when the Spaniards first got wind of them. The Toyopa mines (the Spaniards called them Topira) are located, some say, in the Sierra Madre not far south of the border.[1]

There are many different versions of the Toyopa legend. But they all agree that millions of dollars of gold and silver bullion are buried where the church of Toyopa once stood. Those who have looked for Toyopa — and some claim they have found it — say that the church bells can still be heard when the wind is in the right direction. Others have told of the loud barking of dogs when anyone comes close to the elusive Toyopa. Who knows? The bells of Toyopa might even be heard from the south side of the Huachuca Mountains on a cold, still night. If one listened long enough, surely he would hear the distant sound of barking dogs.

But it would take more than legends of gold to supply the ingot from which Jones whacked off his $890 hunk. It would take real solid metal, glinting in the white light of the Arizona sun. To fit Jones' description, the ingots must have come from an early-day mine — probably a placer or a free-gold one.

The earliest mining in the Southwest was in the 1700's. The Spanish king had given mining grants to a select few who worked the rich surface, or shallow, silver deposits such as those west of Nogales, Arizona — only forty miles from Fort Huachuca. These mines were known as the Planchas de Plata (planks of silver). The rich ore was carried south on the backs of burros to a refinery in Mexico or to some shipping place to be sent to Spain.[2]

In 1774, gold placers were worked at Quijotoa, north of Sells, Arizona, on the Papago Indian Reservation — less than a hundred miles from the fort. In the early 1800's, the mountain men, trapping beavers along the San Pedro and other streams, found some of the rich surface deposits of gold and silver, which were later mined. After the 1850's, gold was produced in great quantities — some of it from Oro Blanco (white gold), within forty miles of Sergeant Jones' treasure. More gold came from Cerro Colorado (red hill), west of the Tucson-Nogales highway. Some came from the Santa Rita Mountains, only twenty-five miles from the fort. In 1858, the rich placers east of Yuma, on the Colorado River, were discovered. By 1873, gold placers were worked at Greaterville, only twenty-five miles from Jones' hole in the ground.

Gold was the most valuable of all minerals produced in the Southwest until 1876, when it took second place to silver (and later, copper), with the discovery of the rich silver mines at Tombstone, on the east side of the San Pedro Valley — just across from Fort Huachuca.

History tells us that there was plenty of mining for real gold — not the legendary variety — taking place not far from the fort, which could have furnished enough bullion to have been stacked like cordwood *if* it had been collected and piled in Jones' hidden room.

Could any of this bullion have found its way to an underground room in the Huachuca Mountains?.

The Huachuca Mountains lie north of the Mexican border, on the west side of the San Pedro Valley. This valley is one of the trailways crossing the Southwest and has been used since man has known that part of

Arizona. Within sight of the Huachucas are two ancient kill sites of mammoth hunters. Along the San Pedro there are also the old campsites of people of the Cochise culture of ten thousand years ago.

The Spaniards were led through this valley in their search for the fabled Seven Cities of Cibola. One of the earliest Spanish settlements in the United States was made at Quiburi in 1696 on the San Pedro. Later the valley was crossed by trails of goldseekers heading west, and it was already well known to the first hardy Americans in the area, the mountain men.

The Butterfield stages followed a trail which crossed the San Pedro at Tres Alamos (three cottonwoods), north of the present city of Benson. Wells-Fargo Express shipped ores from the town of Contention on the San Pedro, first by stage and later by railroad.[3]

The valley has long been a part of the history of the Southwest.[4] But I have never seen any record of any sort of transportation — human, animal, stagecoach, railroad, or auto — that actually carried any bullion to Jones' treasure site. A local mine might have supplied a bar or two, provided there was some reason for hiding the metal. This might have been the case if some rich ores had been high-graded. It would more likely have been free gold mined at nearby placers, stolen and hidden until Jones fell into the hole and found it. Such precious metals were mined in the immediate vicinity, but there is no record of the loss of any bullion in this part of the Southwest which would account for bars "stacked like cordwood."

But there *is* a church record in the town of Mazapil, near Saltillo, Coahuila, Mexico, which tells of such a loss. George Roseveare, a mining engineer with the Arizona Bureau of Mines, told me about it. Mr. Roseveare had lived in Mazapil while mining silver in 1934. He said he had seen records from 1595 showing that a shipment of silver bullion (destined for Mexico City from the Spaniards operating the mine), packed on burros, had never reached its destination. Mazapil is about five hundred miles from Mexico City — it is only a little farther from the Huachuca Mountains. Maybe some of that bullion was taken north.

There is another possibility to account for the treasure. Following the downfall of President Porfirio Díaz in 1910, there were several revolutions in Mexico. Rich landowners in the northern part of the country frequently kept large amounts of gold and silver currency on hand. There are reports that during the revolutions, some persons melted coins into bars, which could be readily taken out of the country or buried until the owners, if lucky enough to survive, could reclaim them. Bars of bullion would not have been convenient to use as money, and they were too difficult to cut up.

"During the height of one revolution," Mr. Roseveare recalled, "the smelter at Mazapil was caught with a great deal of refined silver on hand. Before it closed down, all the refined metal was poured into one great mold that weighed about four thousand pounds. The smelter was one of the first places visited by the rebels and bandits. Whenever we were asked for bullion, we showed them the big hunk and told them to help themselves." He grinned as he recounted, "They always tried to whack off some of the tough metal, but never got enough to pay for a box of cartridges."

If someone did attempt to get a hoard out of Mexico until things settled down, the San Pedro Valley was along the route of one of the oldest trails out of the country. The Huachucas reach to the international border —and Jones' Treasure was found less than fifteen miles away from it.

Some of these places where the bullion might have originated seem a long way from the Huachuca Mountains. However, distances in the days before the railroads really seem to have meant less than now. When it came to hauling minerals from the mines to the place where they could be turned into spending money, hundreds of miles were of little import. Everything mined in the Southwest while it was still a part of Mexico was sent by mule or burro to Mexico City or some other large place such as Guadalajara, Acapulco, or Guaymas on the west coast, and Tampico or Veracruz on the east.

Later, when parts of the Southwest became United States territory, everything mined there found its way to San Francisco. Before railroads came in the 1880's, transportation was by horseback, ox cart, wagon, stagecoach, and steamboat by way of the Gulf of California. Later, when railroads had connected the east and west coasts, ore was also shipped east.

Gold itself was used as currency in the form of nuggets and "dust," to be weighed at the time it passed from the miner to the bartender or to the merchant — not to mention to the charming companions of the dance hall who provided entertainment during leisure hours. There is no record of how much gold accumulated in these ways. Only that which finally reached the mints or the banks has been recorded.

Someone burdened by heavy nuggets and bags of gold dust might have melted down his hoard into handy bars of bullion. There was neither a convenient bank nor a double mattress to trust. A hole in the ground was as safe a hiding place for valuables as could be found.

Life in the Southwest was filled with hazards that are well recorded. First claimed by the Spaniards, parts of the Southwest at some time belonged to Mexico, France, the Republic of Texas, and the Confederacy; parts were threatened by England and Russia. The Southwest was the last of the country to be relinquished by the Indians — the Comanche, Apache, Navajo, and Ute tribes all fought to hold their lands when the rest of the country had long been given up by the other Indian tribes.

Lots of things may have happened in the lives of people — things which were never jotted down by handy diarists, such as how bars of bullion got stacked like cordwood in an underground room in the Huachuca Mountains. But certainly the number of possibilities suggests that gold in this form *could* have reached this hiding place.

Could Sergeant Jones have given a party costing $890 while stationed at Fort Huachuca in 1941?

There is no report of Jones having played such a princely role as host, nor has he ever elaborated on just what kind of party it was. There is no report that the Army or anyone else has ever investigated this phase of his story.

None of the larger towns nearby had much to offer Negro soldiers beyond picture shows and service centers, where they could get coffee, play innocuous games, or read. A party whose tab reached $890 would have been a whing-ding (easily remembered by the police) had it been held in any of these small cities.

But there was that friendly nation to the south — Mexico!

Agua Prieta, just across the border from Douglas and only fifty miles away from the fort, was a preferred recreational area for men in uniform during World War II. While the facilities were somewhat limited — cantinas, fly-specked cafes, curio shops, and a red-light district redolent with the odor of tequila and Tabu — soldiers found it lots more fun, if less elevating culturally, than its sister cities north of the border. Agua Prieta might well have been the setting for the sergeant's $890 party.

There were all sorts of entertainment available, according to Mrs. Annie Hatcher, who operated the International Hotel in Douglas for more than twenty years.

"I don't remember Sergeant Jones ever being at my hotel during the war," she told me, "It was always full of the boys. They sure did enjoy themselves in Mexico, but they quieted down when they stayed at my place. Sergeant Jones and his friends stayed with me while the Army dug for that treasure." She sighed. "I sure hope he finds it."

Lyndon Hargrave, an anthropologist and zoologist who lived at Benson, just forty-five miles from the fort, added to the account.

"I was in and out of all the towns in southern Arizona during the war, while the Negro troops were stationed at the fort — lots of them had their families in Benson — and I never heard of any big parties going on here. But in *Mexico* — I was down there once — I never saw anything like it."

Percy Bowden, who has been chief of police at Douglas for the last thirty-four years, recalled that "during the war, there was a big party going on across the line (in Agua Prieta) all the time. My deputy and I — with the help of the M.P.'s — had to close up the place every night. Sometimes things got pretty noisy."

There is the report of a party that ended up in an international incident at Nogales, Sonora, Mexico, and resulted in the closing of that town to troops. After Nogales, Sonora, had closed up the red-light district, the girls had gone underground and dispersed all over town. It was rumored that after a big drinking party some soldiers had started out to find these ladies and, confusing the addresses, had forced their way into the home of the city's mayor.

Obviously, Jones could have spent his entire wad on a lively party in Mexico — a generous and natural way for a soldier to spend some easily acquired cash. He might just as well have won it in a crap game, I thought, or he might really have found the gold.

Only two people, besides himself, could have given the answer. One of them is dead. The other, the man who bought the gold illegally, hasn't come forward, if indeed he is still alive.

All the single details of Sergeant Jones' story could possibly — by stretching the imagination — have occurred as he told them. Just a few bars, such as those missing from the mine at Mazapil, could seem like a much bigger pile. As for the hole the sergeant fell into — that, too, could have existed. And the $890 party could have been given in the continuous festive mood of the Mexican border towns during the war.

Did it all take place as Jones tells it? Or did the Army's digging prove that Sergeant Jones' Treasure existed only in his imagination?

Before the Army had even filled in the enormous hole it had dug, a friendly bartender in Sierra Vista, a thriving city just outside the gates of the fort, confided in me.

"Sergeant Jones don't know where that treasure's buried."

"No?" I asked.

"They dug in the wrong place. It's in another canyon," he assured me.

Others might start looking for Sergeant Jones Treasure in many different places; but to him — in his own mind — it still lay buried where he had first seen it, and his determination to show it to others had not diminished.

On October 21, 1962, the *Dallas Morning News* announced: "Robert Jones, of Dallas, whose 1959 search for a cache of gold at Ft. Huachuca attracted nationwide attention, has received permission from the Department of the Army to resume his search."

On February 13, 1963, the same paper reported that although Jones himself was seriously ill, arrangements to dig for the gold had been completed:

"A Prescott, Arizona building contractor, Terrell B. Mahan of Mahan Brothers Construction Company, acting for Jones, completed arrangements Tuesday with the Department of the Army to begin digging operations in the search for the cache. He immediately mapped plans to move heavy earth-moving equipment to the site."

The search was on again. By February 21, 1963, things were apparently going so well that the *Gateway Times,* Sierra Vista, Arizona, was quite enthusiastic. "Grace McCool believes Jones Will Find Gold," its headline read. It reported that the value of the cache was at least $90,000,000 — a nice round figure. Its origin was ascribed to the notorious Estrada gang, who — according to the ever-ready source, a legend — had sacked the city of Monterrey, Mexico, in 1881.

Monterrey, in the late 1800's, was a prosperous trading center with a federal mint, a gold and silver smelter, a cathedral rich in golden communion plates and holy figurines, and a bank crammed full of coins and

— John Riddick, *Tucson Daily Citizen*

"FACT OR FABLE, JONES GOLD AT BRINK OF 'FINAL TEST.'"So the *Tucson Daily Citizen* reported on February 26, 1963, in relating the search made by the Mahan brothers for Sergeant Jones' treasure.

In this picture water is being pumped from the hole excavated by a bulldozer and a large backhoe used in digging for the treasure.

gold bars. The thieves, according to the tale, made a successful getaway with their loot, leaving a bloody trail in their wake all the way to Arizona, where they planned to return and "live-it-up" in the booming, wide-open town of Tombstone. As happens so often, a little misunderstanding arose within the gang. Those who survived were later caught and killed, but not until one had told his story, starting a treasure hunt that has since covered most of southeastern Arizona.

The bloody trail of the murderers must have been wiped out by the tracks of burros needed to haul off the ninety-million-dollar loot. Even if each animal had been loaded with 180 pounds — a pretty heavy load for a donkey — there would have been a thousand burros hauling off the estimated 180,000 pounds of bullion, coins, and jewels. Bloody or not, the trail should have been well worn!

"No one has searched the Huachuca Canyon for the loot buried so long ago until Sergeant Jones told his story," the *Times* continued. "It is there."

In the same issue of the *Times,* progress in the search was reported with glittering details. "The Daniels twins, Ina and Nina, are secretaries for Jones and are keeping a written report on happenings. To date, they have thirty-five chapters written about the gold hunt. The attractive twins are dressed in gold, use gold ball-point pens, and write with gold ink."

On February 26, 1963, a special article by staff writer John Riddick, in the *Tucson Daily Citizen,* told of efforts by C. O. Mitchell, an Apache Junction prospector, to use a metal-detecting device at the excavation. "After turning on his instrument," Riddick reported, Mitchell shouted, "'Thunderation, you're sitting right on it!'"

Among others who believed Jones' story was his spiritual advisor, Mitchell Holland. "The spirit showed me in a vision where the gold is and that's where they are digging now," he was reported as saying. Three of Jones' friends were also on hand to watch out for his interests — and they, too, expressed faith in Jones' story.

Also keeping an eye on the progress were the government representatives from the Adjutants General Office, with an organization on the ground, called Project Research, ready to take charge of the treasure as soon as it was uncovered.

Riddick's story continued: "Arizona contractor Terrell Mahan has staked all his money on faith that Jones' vision is in the ground as well as in his head. Now at the end of his purse string, Mahan says he'll have to quit if one more hole doesn't produce the gold. And Mahan's brother, Gordon, said, 'I'll believe the gold is there, even if we don't find it.' Another of Jones' friends added, 'He won't quit if we don't find it now.'"

"Others won't either," Riddick concluded. "Dreams of treasure die hard in the mind of man. A legend has been created here and if the gold is not found this week, it will bring others to this canyon later."

The gold wasn't found, but the search for it will go on. It has been reported that Jones received permission directly from the White House to dig for his treasure, but the next searcher may not receive so favorable a response to hunt for treasure on the military reservation.

The Army's effort and that of the Mahans made me wonder. Why had Sergeant Jones created a legend so realistic to himself and to others? Could it be an unconscious assembling of many facts, briefly glimpsed or heard, which fell into place in his mind and emerged as a fully reasonable account?

There are literally hundreds of abandoned mines in the Southwest. There are active copper smelters, with their bars of bright metal stacked like cordwood. Could these sights, along with the many tales of buried treasures, have provided a foundation for his story? Had he embellished it with added details about a fabulous party? Since his sincerity seemed beyond question, could his treasure have been the unwitting trick of imagination born of hopeless longing for wealth?

One thing is certain — there wasn't any treasure where Sergeant Jones told the Army and the Mahans to dig.

The search for Sergeant Jones' Treasure then answered my question as to HOW a legend might have been created — only by posing two others: WHY are legends created and WHAT brings them about? Had I been told of legends of buried treasure and lost mines in answer to my inquiries about archaeology because of some kinship between treasure hunters and archaeologists? Were we all seeking something that is never found?

All of the true story that is hidden in archaeology will never be known. There are only the artifacts themselves and the related information from other fields of research — ethnology, history, paleontology, geology — from which the archaeologist must reconstruct, with imagination, what these facts signify. They will never tell how the people who made and used the things archaeologists dig up actually lived; their looks, their thoughts, their conversations. No matter how full the information, the interpretation is always relative, depending on the archaeologist's knowledge (his own and others) at the time and on his own experience.

The more the archaeologist discovers, the less he knows, for with each new discovery more questions will arise. The only certainty is that the future, with more information, will call for better interpretations.

But what I learned from Sergeant Jones' search for his treasure made me eager to look for the answer to my questions in other legends and visions of treasure that I had already known.

Pots of Gold

HOW A FEW FACTS can be turned into a lot of fantasy is shown by the story of the Pots of Gold. The first I heard about it was just before World War II, when I was doing some archaeological work in southeastern Arizona, not far from Mexico.

The story, however, had its beginning in 1933. At that time, I was making an intensive survey of Chihuahua for Gila Pueblo, to locate remains of the Hohokam, the ancient farmers of the Arizona desert.

How much territory the Hohokam — meaning the "old ones" in the Pima-Papago language — had once called their own had not been determined. Little was known of the archaeology of northern Mexico, except for the great house ruins at Casas Grandes, west of Chihuahua City. Nearby were rock shelters in which stone and adobe houses had been built, some with great beehive-shaped storage bins, made like giant baskets covered with cement-like adobe. In the rugged canyons of the Sierra Madre, were some spectacular cliff houses, much like those in other parts of the Southwest. What else the country held had yet to be discovered.

So, early in 1933, I went to Chihuahua with a permit from the Mexican government that gave me six months to cover the state. The country was still restless from the latest revolution, when many of the large land holdings had been taken over and parceled out in small lots to the farmers. The state of Chihuahua was far from the seat of the federal government at Mexico City, but it was run most efficiently by General Rodrigo M. Quevedo, acting governor. Soldiers were stationed in every community, and the politicians who were in office wore their side arms openly.

Since most of my life had been spent in the Southwest, I already knew something of the Mexican people and how they ticked. First, I got a letter from a friend, who was a friend of the general's, introducing me to him. With this, I finally got one from the general, not only giving me his personal permit to carry on archaeologically, but recommending me to all others in the state for like treatment.

In remote regions, and Chihuahua had many of them in 1933, I showed my letter of introduction until I found someone to help me, usually the *Presidente Municipal* — the local head of the civil government. *El Presidente* often had me wait while he called his "secretary." And when some young man appeared in tow of one of the youngsters who had

27

crowded about my car, he read the general's letter aloud to a curious group now gathered about us.

After much discussion, in which *El Presidente* was the main participant, the secretary would tell me, "Tomorrow, come back tomorrow." Then I would be given a letter to the military commander who might be in another town. By this time, I was becoming well known in the neighborhood as that *Norteamericano* who asked so many questions about the ancient ones.

I never lacked for guides. Eventually, someone always showed up claiming to know where the old places were and how to get there. Sometimes there were more guides than I could find room for, crowded on top of the metal body of my Model A Ford. When I started out, with the springs pressed flat to the axles, slowly driving along the ruts that served for wagon roads, I could depend on some of my riders dropping off at the first settlement we reached. I might even find myself without guides, but there were others willing to take their places for a ride farther on. When I finally arrived at my destination, sometimes it was to discover that the ancient ruins were nothing but a long-abandoned ranch house, its adobe walls still standing.

Wide smiles and gesturing hands tried to assure me that treasures surely could be found here. Buried treasures must be what I was really after!

In time, soldiers proved to be the best guides. They were not going for a visit, and usually they were anxious to return to their stations where their wives prepared their meals — the kind of food I carried lacked the beans and tortillas they preferred.

Wherever I asked about ruins, I showed the samples of Hohokam pottery I carried. It is unlike any other pottery of the Southwest with its decorations in red paint and paste filled with mica. When the Mexicans looked it over, they shook their heads and passed the pieces of broken pottery *(tepelcates)* around, turning them so that the bright sunlight made the mica in the dull clay glisten like gold.

The trash mounds, particularly, of the old villages had been sought and found. Only a little shoveling was needed to tell how rich in *tepelcates* they might be. The depth of the trash was of even greater interest. If it had accumulated during the passing of many years, its story would be told in the different kinds of pottery that had been made at different times — the latest at the top and the oldest at the bottom. In tests of this sort, all pieces of pottery were carefully screened from the black earth of the mounds. The sherds (fragments of pottery) were sacked along with the few artifacts of bone, shell, and stone that might be found. Each sack was marked to show the depth from which its contents had come and each ruin located on a map.

All of this activity was watched by a wide-eyed audience that gathered in some mysterious manner out of the open spaces. First there would be two or three young boys who sat watching from the back of a burro they had ridden from out of nowhere. If the work went on for a few hours, there was certain to be a circle of young men, squatting about the test pit as we went deeper and filled more paper sacks. Whenever it was necessary to camp overnight to finish some work, the audience swelled even more the next day. By this time, the old men had joined the others. There might even be some women, who hung back of those who crowded close, noting each object that was saved and sacked.

I had long given up trying to explain that I was interested only in the broken pieces of old pottery, that I did not care to go to some other place and dig for lost treasure, no matter how much my visitors insisted that they could point out places more promising in riches. Finally the bystanders gave up — they were busy telling each other about their own legends of lost treasures.

Frequently, I heard tales of another *Norteamericano* who had been to the places where I dug.

"Looking for ruins?"

"No, señor. He talked only of gold and silver."

I thought of the late J. Frank Dobie, who had written stories of buried treasures and lost mines in the Southwest after hearing some of the same stories I had been told. By retelling the tales in his books, he had produced real gold and silver for himself. It was difficult to make the same people, who must have told their legends to him, believe that I was only looking for *tepelcates*.

When my work in Chihuahua was finished, I had collected several truckloads of sherds from different parts of the state, and the results showed that the more one finds out about the past, the less one knows. There were more questions raised than answered. To answer some of these new questions, I went to southern Arizona five years later, and there I heard about the Pots of Gold.

It was in the little border town of Naco, on a rainy November afternoon in 1938. My work was close by, so I had made Bisbee, north of the border, my headquarters. There I could find Mexican miners, temporarily out of work, to help with the excavations that had come as a result of my earlier work in Chihuahua. Not only were the miners good at moving dirt, but they were also pleasant to be with; their talk usually turned to tales of many things, mostly to legends of lost treasures and mines.

It was one of those autumnal rainy spells that soak the Arizona desert. Impatiently, I spent another long day hoping that the cold rain would stop so the work could go on. Naco did not have much to offer the visitor — one street of three blocks of curio shops, cafes, a leather shop, and some general stores. I had wandered in and out of them, when the heavy mist turned to a drizzle that sent me into a nearby cantina. The long, narrow room had a small bar alongside one wall. A couple of windows let in the dim light from outside. Two tables, covered with red oil cloth, were near a pot-bellied stove. It was more decorative than useful, until someone stuffed in a piece of cardboard or a twisted newspaper, stirring up the half-burned fuel. But its presence was a kind of welcome on a bleak day in the high altitude. At least the cantina was a place to sit and sip a tequila sour, a satisfying Mexican drink, softened with lime juice and water, with a dash of syrup — fine either on a cold, dreary day, or a hot, sultry one.

I sat alone until a Mexican, about my age, came in and sat at the adjoining table. He was dressed in the brown cottons of the country people, and he looked more like one of them than a border town resident, who rarely wore the short work jacket and sturdy cotton trousers. A white hat of finely woven palm fronds was tilted back from his broad forehead. His high cheek bones and square jaws made his face seem broader, but fitting with his stocky body.

He had brought with him one of those small, unlabeled bottles in which native drinks were then sold in little Mexican bars. Beside the bottle, he placed the halves of a large green lime and a small square of newspaper holding a mound of salt. He invited me to join him as he took a swig from the bottle, followed by a lick of salt he had placed on his left fist, and then by a quick suck of the bitter lime juice. I held up my glass, as I preferred my fiery Mexican tequila watered down, and asked him to join me.

He pulled up a chair and I told him my name. He said I could call him Rod and told me that he was waiting for a ride to the mining town of Cananea, which was near where he had been working. Soon I knew he was different from so many of the people one met in border towns at that time, particularly as a chance acquaintance in a bar. Too often I had found myself, under similar circumstances, tied to an over-demonstrative drunk who insisted that I drink *his* way. Or I was besieged by a seller of obscene postcards, or cheap jewelry, or even hollowed-out pecans made into pigs whose ears and tails were wiggled by the captive flies within.

Rod told me that he had worked in the States, along the border and even in Los Angeles. He preferred to live in Mexico, though he could not find work easily. Before I could tell him something of myself, he said, "You dig for things, I have heard."

"Yes, I'm an archaeologist," I explained.

"I know, for I have sometimes been in Bisbee. It must be a lot of gold you look for—"

"No," I interrupted him, "archaeologists don't look for gold." I could feel that he was like so many others I had run across in the Southwest. No need to try to explain that the pieces of pottery, old bones, and rocks that archaeologists dug up were the things we really wanted.

"There are many treasures," he mused.

"I know," I told him. "I think I've heard of them all. But I've never seen any of the real stuff, or known anyone who has. They are just legends — stories."

"I know of one that was found in Mexico," he told me.

That would be different, I thought, for although I had heard of many people looking for treasure, I had never talked to anyone who had actually found any.

While I listened, he told me that he was born near a little town northwest of Chihuahua City. I tried to remember this part of the state. As he talked, I recalled bit by bit that his town of San Buenaventura was in the Santa María Valley, where I had spent a great deal of time. It was filled with archaeological sites, one of which had been thoroughly tested because of its deep trash mounds.

"Many of my people lived there," he said, settling himself down to what I felt would be a long story. He spoke of the big ranches and farms in the valley he had known as a boy. Some of his Indian ancestors had lived there long before the Spaniards had come to Mexico.

"My mother told us the stories her grandmother had told her. Her people lived as they always had, grinding corn, weaving serapes, making pottery. They were most proud of the pottery for they never traded it. There was much pottery in the house of my grandmother's people."

Rod told me there were many things that his ancestors knew that the Spanish who came to work the Chihuahua mines wanted to find out. There was the gold that his grandmother's people kept in little skin bags that were always passed from father to son. No one knew where the gold had come from. Then the Spanish came with their soldiers and said they must take the gold for their king. But the gold was gone, and though the soldiers watched night and day, they never found it.

Rod finished his little bottle, rolled a corn husk cigarette, and told how the soldiers had taken all the corn and burned the houses. They broke all the pottery and left the people nothing but the clothes they wore.

"That is what my grandmother told me, and it must be true," he concluded.

"But what about the treasure that was found?"

Digressions are normal with those who tell of lost treasures. Sometimes these are more interesting than the main story. I had expected to hear another version of the stories of pots filled with gold coins or nuggets, buried and now sought with the aid of a clue provided in a forked tree trunk. The clues are identical everywhere I heard the story, from Parral in Chihuahua to southeastern New Mexico and even into the Panhandle of Texas. There the legend may have died for lack of trees needed to furnish clues.

Rod rolled another cigarette before he answered, "Only my family ever knew of the gold."

I could vouch for that, since all the time spent in the Santa María Valley, I could not recall any stories such as his.

"Were you living there in 1933?" I asked.

"No, my family left after the revolution of 1928. But now I can speak of the gold, for it has been found and taken away."

"You see, my grandmother's people put the gold into the clay used for making the pottery. There it was, all the time the soldiers were looking for it. When the people went away, the broken pottery with the gold in it was left behind."

He sighed. "Only they knew this. Before they could go back to where they had lived, no one any longer remembered exactly where it was, except that it was on the west bank of the river."

"Did you ever look for it?" I asked.

"When I was young. We looked many times. But no more. A man came and took it all away."

"How do you know?"

"My cousin told me. He saw the man. Four, five years ago. He filled many bags with the broken pottery and carried it away."

"Why didn't your cousin stop him?"

"There was a soldier with him. He had a letter from the general. He had a map, he knew where to look!"

I was thinking. Five years ago, San Buenaventura — I had been there. It was one of the places where we had spent a week or more.

"Are you sure he found the gold in pieces of broken pottery?"

"Of course. Afterwards, when my cousin told me, we dug where the man had dug. He must have taken it all. We found nothing but the kind of pottery that's everywhere."

"Why do you think it was gold he was digging for?"

Rod shrugged. "Why else would he come with a soldier to dig, and then carry away broken pieces of pottery, filling so many sacks that made a big load for the little truck? My cousin tried to climb on, but he fell off."

What he told me was just as I remembered it! There was a ruin with deep trash near San Buenaventura with lots of pottery. The samples of Hohokam pottery, with its mica glittering like gold specks in the sunlight, had been shown to all who had come to watch. The truck had been over-

A LEGEND OF POTS OF GOLD came from our digging in the deep trash mounds (at the left of the picture) beyond our camp in the Santa María Valley of Chihuahua.

This archaeological site had been shown to us by soldier guides from the town of San Buenaventura. As we screened for artifacts — mainly broken pieces of pottery — the number of visitors increased the longer we worked. They became more curious as we filled many paper sacks with potsherds in our search for Hohokam pottery made with mica-filled clay that glittered like gold.

loaded with two soldiers perching on top — and I remembered that someone had tried to climb on and was shoved off as we drove away. He ran after us, hollering, while the soldiers laughed at him.

All those things were true!

"But there wasn't any gold!" I tried helplessly to interrupt him, although I knew that he would never be convinced that archaeologists looked only for things like broken pottery.

This was a new experience for me. A legend had been built around me — at least in part. I wondered if Rod had created it just to fit the facts: digging in the Santa María Valley, my showing and asking about bits of pottery that seemed to be filled with gold specks, soldiers, a letter from the general, and all the sacks of sherds carefully saved and carried away.

"Look, señor," he said, and drew a thin square of paper from his pocket, a Mexican lottery ticket printed in a delicate shade of blue. "This," he explained, "cost me one peso. And it makes me a rich man."

"The drawing's a month from now," I told him, as I read the date on the ticket and wondered what this had to do with the story he had just told me.

"Certainly," he answered, "But I have thought many times of all the things I could do if I won."

"And if you lose?"

He laughed. "Then I will think how good it is not to have to take care of all those things I would have bought."

"Don't you want to be rich?"

"Maybe. None of my friends are rich."

"What about this gold you told me about?"

"My family has always known of the pots of gold. We have thought of the things we would have when we found them. That has given us much pleasure."

"But if you knew no gold was found, wouldn't you want to know about it?"

"No, señor. It's better to be happy thinking about something you don't have, than to have it and be unhappy. Anyway, if that man didn't find the broken pots of gold, they must be some other place."

Maybe that is how legends are kept alive. There is more pleasure and excitement in the search and anticipation of the find, than could ever come from the finding!

Was Rod's story of the Pots of Gold one he had created to fit the facts his cousin had told him? I knew I had not heard the story while I dug in Mexico. He had made it seem so real that I'm sure that if I had heard it then — even though it would have struck me as just another legend — I would have looked a little harder for pottery glittering like gold. Maybe some pottery-maker had done just what Rod said his grandmother's people had done so long ago.

It could have happened!

A Lost Mountain of Uranium

ROD'S TALE of the Pots of Gold convinced me that my search for Hohokam pottery (which I never found) in the Santa María Valley had been interpreted by him or his cousin as others had often done: that I was actually looking for buried treasure and not for archaeological artifacts. I thought he had invented the rest of the story to account for the "treasure" I had found and carried away.

On the other hand, our digging might have been interpreted to fit an existing legend, such as Rod related, although I was certain I had never heard his particular legend while I was in Mexico. Anyhow, I still lacked a full answer to my question, how is a legend started?

It was more than ten years after I heard Rod's tale, that I seemed closer to an answer. In 1950, as curator of the Arizona State Museum, my time was no longer spent entirely as a field archaeologist, though I continued to carry on some research. By that time, the greater part of the Southwest had been covered by archaeological surveys. Many important digs had been completed, on some of which I had worked.

Thirty years had passed since I had started my survey of Texas and, later, parts of New Mexico, Arizona, and Mexico. During this time, I had made many trips that carried me to the west coast, into the plains, and east into the Mississippi Valley, to see first hand what other archaeologists were doing. A great deal of territory had been covered, for the Southwest is a large region.

When I had started my work, shortly after World War I, highways barely existed in parts of the country. On some of the big ranches, roads lost themselves at a lonely little house, a windmill, or a water tank. Then the traveler either had to backtrack or strike out across the country looking for another road or trail to follow.

In the country west of the Pecos River, some kind of mountain was always in sight, somewhere on the horizon, unless one happened to be in the midst of a dense forest or deep canyon. And unless one was stopped by a large river, the desert country had always been a fairly easy one to cross, even without well-defined roads.

Author's note: At the request of some of those involved, the names of people and places in this account of the Lost Mountain of Uranium have been modified in order to conceal identity.

During the dry season, and most of the Southwest is always dry, one could go many places, away from the main roads, by following the ridges to avoid crossing the sandy washes. These usually lost their steep banks when they reached the valley floor where the stream beds spread into gravel fans. Or there were deep arroyos where erosion had cut miniature canyons in the silty valleys.

Another way to travel was in these washes themselves. Once a track had been marked in the gravel and sand of the dry stream bed, it remained until an occasional flood wiped it out. Then a new set would be made by the first traveler to go that way.

The people who had lived for many years on the land knew how to get from place to place without roads. These were the people from whom archaeological information was sought. And sometimes, a tale of buried treasures or a lost mine was included in the answers. It always brought to mind the question, just how and why does a legend come to life?

I came closer to the answer on a hot summer afternoon in 1950 under a wide-spreading cottonwood tree in West Texas. I had made a visit to my old home town, which I had left twenty years earlier. Among my friends was one whom I always thought of as "Dutch," though I never called him by that name. His accent was different from that of the drawling Texans, and his verbs always came near the ends of his sentences.

He had shown up as an overgrown boy at the end of World War I, when everyone with an accent was still suspect. He never explained how he happened to be in West Texas, working as a roustabout, a cook, a bronco-buster. He could do just about anything. Even if he were an escaped German prisoner of war, as some thought, his past was his own as long as he conformed to the ways of his adopted country.

"All I want is a chance to work," he once told me.

Everyone who knew him was glad to give him that chance. When the oil boom of the 1920's struck that part of Texas, Dutch worked for a while as a roughneck, drilling wells. Or he worked as a carpenter, for he could build a house alone, even putting up the heavy ridge plate, the rafters and studding. Then he went back to the cattle country.

There he acquired a little piece of land — by marrying the grand-daughter of the nester who had settled on it before the ranches were fenced. But he often left his wife alone in the little shack her grandfather had built, while he was away working for the cash they needed. He was always being called to do a job that others said could not be done. The harder the work and the more skill it required, the better Dutch liked it.

His intelligence fitted him to do more than manual labor. He could have worked up to a responsible position in almost any of the industries that were developing in West Texas. But maintaining a home on his tiny piece of land seemed to be his only goal.

The little house was hidden in an orchard of peach and plum trees. The seep spring that trickled from the rocky land into the little valley of rich black soil ended in a pool at the foot of a big cottonwood. Dutch developed a fine flow of water, which he directed into a two-inch pipe that ran into an open ditch just outside the kitchen door. His lush garden attracted all the jack rabbits within miles, and there was more than enough water for the little swimming pool under the tree. There was even a shower, enclosed with burlap sacks, supplied by a fifty-gallon metal tank on a platform overhead, providing warm water when the sun was shining.

"The simple life, we have," he told me the last time I had seen him. Now he was having trouble with the owner of the ranch that surrounded his little place. The water he had developed and used to irrigate his garden and fill his pool could have watered many head of cattle.

Dutch and his wife put up with cut fences and stray cattle that trampled their gardens whenever they were away. Sometimes the sound of a shot in the darkness frightened his wife when she was alone. Still they managed to hang on, while his spring of water had become almost as valuable as the oil that had been discovered on the rancher's land. Before the oil field could be developed, Dutch had made a deal to supply the water to drill the wells in exchange for a clear title to his homesite and a substantial income.

Dutch and his wife had lived in town while the wells had been drilled and had leased their little place to the developer. He had fixed it up with all sorts of conveniences — running water, an electric light plant — and had added rooms for a kitchen and bath.

Now Dutch and his wife had returned, and he was working harder than ever, doing things he could have well afforded to have someone else do. His wife was even busier, planting wild flowers in the rock terraces he had built and taking care of all the modern gadgets.

With all the changes that had taken place in their financial circumstances, their ways had not changed. Dutch still did the cooking when "company" came, as he had always done. It was just as relaxing as ever to sit under the big cottonwood tree, sipping one of his tall highballs and admiring the mass of colorful flowers his wife raised. There was time to talk about the years he had spent on ranches, in oil fields, and, during the Depression, cutting lawns. We talked of his struggle to hold his little patch of land and of the newest projects he planned.

Among these projects Dutch was then in the midst of hunting for uranium. He was working, he said, for someone who owned a claim on the Navajo Indian Reservation in the Luka-chu-kai Mountains of Arizona.

After one of his recent trips there, he had brought back some of the uranium-bearing carnotite — pale yellow rocks with streaks of orange. There was a pile of them between our reclining canvas chairs, and on it sat a Geiger counter, clicking like a runaway clock.

"Next you'll strike it rich in uranium," I told him.

"Before that time, I sell out," he answered. "I only like to look."

As the afternoon shortened, a gentle breeze rustled the leaves overhead, and the bright sunlight slipped under the long branches and spotted the green grass with patches of yellow. Overhead, the orange and yellow orioles fussed as they fluttered about their hanging nests, and the black cow birds shrilled back at them. The Geiger counter clicked away loudly on the pile of lemon-yellow ore. The bright rays from the lowering sun finally reached under the spreading limbs of the cottonwood, and struck full force on the hunks of ore. There they glowed yellow and orange, rivaling the orioles in the leaves above.

Soon the aroma of Dutch's thick steaks and fried potatoes from his outside grill drove other thoughts from my mind. But as we ate, I could not keep my eyes away from that pile of ore or shut out the sound of the Geiger counter.

For days after I had returned to Arizona, I kept remembering the brightly colored rocks. The memory was hauntingly familiar. Then it came to me in a flash! Bright yellow and orange, black and brown — a mountainside of bright-colored rocks. Where had I seen it?

Somewhere there was a mountain cliff with colors like those of the carnotite ore. I thought of the Navajo country, where carnotite had been used by the Indians for generations as the yellow pigment for their sand paintings. But I had never done any archaeological work there, other than to visit the Basketmaker Caves in the red sandstone cliffs of the deep canyons. I recalled mainly the drives across the flat sagebrush and juniper mesas and the camps at the foot of the pine-covered mountains.

I knew it had to be in a mountainous region, for the cliff was of mountain size, not just an outcropping of rock. Mentally, I retraced my tracks during the past, over much of Western Texas, New Mexico, Arizona, and northern Mexico. Finally, I narrowed the area to that part of the Southwest that was west of the Pecos River, but including northern Mexico.

During the months that followed, I checked and re-checked my old field notes. But I could find no clue that led to the yellow cliff. The more I thought of it, the clearer all the little things became that had happened before and after I had seen it. The road, in particular, that had led to it.

It was the sort of road that is not easily forgotten, although it was like many others in some ways. There were only two deep car tracks in a

DOES A MOUNTAIN OF URANIUM ORE lie somewhere to the south or west of El Capitán in the Guadalupe Mountains? A rocky cliff is the spot, such as that to the right in the picture, which once turned to bright yellow in the light of a setting sun. A set of lonely tracks in a sandy wash leads to it, just as the end of the rainbow pinpoints a pot of gold.

broad, sandy arroyo bed, leading off the main road that we had followed. They were as well marked as if a car had gone on ahead moments before. But they might have been made a year earlier. There was no sign of any flooding in the dry stream bed, no tight wedging of driftwood against the low-growing shrubs, no sharp rippling on the sand banks, and no animal tracks in the loose, dry silt piled against the larger boulders.

We had followed the tracks to look for archaeological sites. And then, because there was no way to get out or turn around in the wash, we kept on. We spent the large part of a day driving slowly, stopping to look on the higher land beyond the banks. There the ground was covered with dry, brittle grass and the scrub growth of cat-claw, with its sparse foliage that snatched at our clothing as we brushed past. It was the sort of country where little of archaeological interest could be expected. The dry wash we were following was the largest nearby drainage from the mountain range ahead. Finally we gave up looking as the country became even drier, and just drove on. The tracks went on for mile after mile, as the draw wound its way in sweeping curves.

It was long past mid-afternoon when the tracks finally climbed a low earthen bank on which some scrubby hackberry trees grew. There the level ground, sloping from a massive front of bare rock, was spotted with dusty weeds, and, near the clump of trees, were two army squad tents, with framed sidewalls and peaked roofs. The khaki-colored canvas hung in strips from the bare rafters.

Inside one tent was a work bench with hand tools, metal buckets, and cans of nails, bolts, and nuts. Everything was covered with a heavy film of dust-colored grease. The other tent, floored with rough wooden planks half-covered by fine sand, contained a built-in plank table and an open cupboard, containing cans of coffee, flour, and sugar, stacks of tin plates and cups, and a can filled with knives, forks, and spoons. Beyond the cupboard was a flat-topped, wood-burning iron stove with two round lids. The lifter was still in one of them, and a big black iron kettle sat on the back of the stove. The two corners of the tent, along the back wall, were filled with wooden bunks.

Outside, there were scattered lengths of wire cable, some broken shovels and picks, and parts of iron wheels, axles, and bent frames. All seemed to have been left as though the owners might return at any time. But the dust-covered interiors and tattered condition of the tents showed that they must have left long ago.

When we had come to the end of the tracks, it was too late to think of returning down the wash for a dry overnight camp in the sandy arroyo. So we made camp near the stream bed, and away from the two tents where a rattlesnake might come from under the floor boards in the cool of the night.

Although nothing of archaeological promise had been found on the trip, I decided to take some pictures of the abandoned camp to add to my file. The massive wall of rocks behind the tents made a good background and by the time I had photographed them, the sun had lowered until dark shadows had crept up the face of the cliff. It had become a mass of bright yellows and oranges, with streaks of moss green. The colors on the mountainside stood out like some abstract painting, framed by the deep blue sky above and the darkening shadows below. Just to look at all that color was enough to repay me for the long, hot trip up the dry stream bed.

The next morning we left at sunup. The return to the main road was hurried, but we spent another long, hot day in the stream bed before we camped for the night. So I remembered this road more than others.

Now, as I tried to place it, I recalled, too, how we sometimes had to keep going for days before we found a camping place with enough water and shade for a good rest. Then I could write up my notes in full. This was the routine that I had followed while making the archaeological survey of the Southwest, over a period of thirty years. Sometimes, it was only a trip for a few days; sometimes, for weeks or months, covering as much of the country as could be reached by car, on horseback, or by foot. We made camp where night might catch us, as on the trip up the dry wash. Only when we found a camping place with all the water we needed could we develop the negatives that had been exposed. We used a "change" bag to place the exposed roll of film in a section of inner tube that served for a developing tank. The chemicals had to be chilled at night by wrapping the bottles in damp cloths so that evaporation would cool them.

I seemed to recall that, after this particular trip, the negative of the abandoned tents and the colorful cliff was fogged, just black. And I remember that this also happened with another roll, so the unused ones were thrown away. Perhaps, I thought at the time, they had been bought at some small town where they might have been in stock too long, or maybe precautions had not been taken to keep them from the heat, or the developer had gone bad.

Anyway, I had forgotten the trip up the dry wash. Thirty years after I had started looking for archaeological sites, it had all come back to me. The yellow-orange cliff on the mountainside, like the color of the ore at Dutch's; the road up the dry wash; the abandoned prospector's camp, and, especially, the photographic film that was clouded.

What I saw must have been an entire mountain of carnotite, such as Dutch had looked for in the Navajo country on the Colorado Plateau of northeastern Arizona. The photographic negative must have been clouded by ore rich in uranium!

It gradually dawned on me that I had the making of a legend of my own! A Mountain of Uranium — somewhere in the Southwest! What was I to do with it?

First, I tried to forget it. I was sure it was only the association of many different things and places I had seen in the past thirty years, maybe even before that. The clicking Geiger counter at Dutch's place, the pile of ore, brilliant yellow and orange in the late sunlight, had brought them all together. It couldn't be true, no matter how much it seemed so to me.

But just try to forget something like a bright yellow-orange colored mountainside — especially if it *might* be some kind of uranium ore. Even though it must have been my imagination, everything in the desert country reminded me of the yellow cliff — the blooming *palo verde* that dotted the whole desert each May with splashes of yellow and green and the yellow asters in the summer. The harder I tried to forget it all, the more firmly fixed became each detail of the trip up the dry wash, the abandoned camp, the cliff of yellow and orange rock, and the fogged film.

Finally, I decided to run it down, to find the place where the tents had stood beneath the cliff, and so to clear it all from my mind. But when I came to look for the place on a map, I had nothing sure to guide me. Had I failed to record a place and an incident because it had added nothing to the archaeological record? More likely, the fact that my field notes had nothing to show meant that the yellow cliff and the road up the dry wash were two different things. Or that they didn't exist at all.

But again, the harder I tried to forget it, the more firmly fixed the image became. I determined to keep it all to myself until I was sure it actually didn't exist. With better maps than I had used in the field, I began to eliminate those parts of the Southwest where the mountain and dry wash could not possibly exist. There remained the western side of the Guadalupe Mountains that extend from Texas into New Mexico, halfway between the Pecos River and the Rio Grande. Then there was southwestern New Mexico, southeastern Arizona, and some of northern Chihuahua; and finally, and most likely, the Big Bend country of Texas. All together, this is an area of about three hundred by six hundred miles, approximately the size of the northeastern United States including Pennsylvania. At least there were some places on the map which might contain the kind of dry washes that I had followed. The image of the lost mountain of uranium I kept to myself, for I felt that I had merely put together bits of fact and come up with a full-blown vision of my own. But the fantasy was so real that when finally I told it to a friend who was passing through Tucson, a West Texas oil man who owned a private plane, he said,

"Let's look for it. We'll fly over the whole country.'

"It really doesn't exist," I protested. "I just, well . . . it can't be. I've checked my notes and maps."

"Maybe it does. Anyway, it will be fun to look."

Before we could get around to it, the federal government stopped offering a bonus for new discoveries in uranium, and since it was the only purchaser of the mineral, uranium mines were no longer in urgent demand. There was now no excuse — even for the "fun of it" — to look for something I felt sure I had only imagined — a yellow cliff of carnotite. And so our search was halted before it had begun.

Years afterwards, I told Dutch about my mountain of carnotite, lost somewhere in the desert country of the Southwest. His blue eyes twinkled as I told him of the time I had spent running through my notes, checking maps, trying to find some place where a road up a dry wash *could* lead toward the east to a mountain.

"Carnotite," he chuckled. "No carnotite except in the Colorado Plateau has ever been found."

"Only the Navajo country?"

"And in Colorado."

"Then I could have saved myself all that work!"

"You sure could if you had checked your geology." (I have since done so.) My colors on the cliff must have gone away with the sun — nothing but sunlight on a rock cliff!

So, I thought, it must have all come to life on a balmy afternoon in the shade of his cottonwood tree, while sipping some mighty tall whiskies, with the sound of a clicking Geiger counter on a pile of yellow ore that had been turned to bright orange by a Texas sun.

Dry arroyos, roads no longer traveled that led to abandoned camps, films spoiled by the heat, and mountains turned to gold by a setting sun were all as real as the Southwest that I had seen. The vision of the Lost Mountain of Uranium had been created out of these. I knew that my fantasy was made up of unrelated facts, and I knew now that there could be no carnotite where I had looked on the maps for the yellow cliff, but WHY had I created this fantasy?

The lost mountain had become as real to me as the truest experience, and the more I tried to forget it, the more firmly it stuck. And should I ever happen to see that dry wash with the tracks in it, I would want to follow them. Of course, only to make sure at least that there is really no mountain of uranium at the end of the trail!

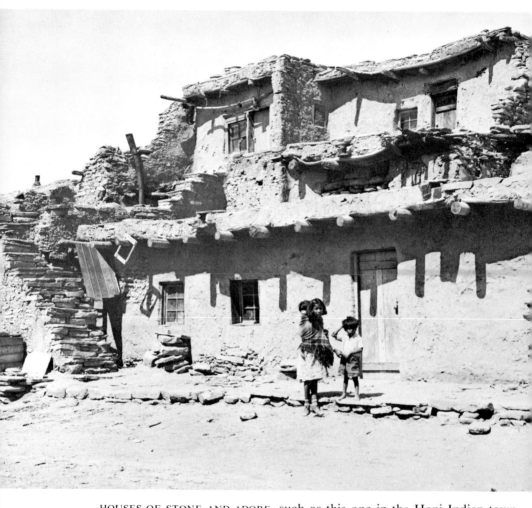

HOUSES OF STONE AND ADOBE, such as this one in the Hopi Indian town of Oraibi in northern Arizona, were discovered by Coronado instead of the cities he had set out to find — cities larger and richer than any in Mexico.

Back of It All

Of all those who talked of and sought wealth in the New World, no one was so instrumental in creating treasure legend as a man called Cowshead — Alvar Nuñez Cabeza de Vaca — who came to America in 1528.[5] He and his companions, Castillo Maldonado, Andrés Dorantes, and his Negro slave, Estevan, were the only survivors of the Spanish expedition of Panfilio de Narváez which landed on the coast of Florida to explore the land north of the Gulf of Mexico — with high hopes of finding great riches. Unfortunately, all the ships were wrecked somewhere along the coast of Texas during a spell of what now is referred to as "severe" weather.

After eight years, Cabeza de Vaca and his three companions managed to make their way across the entire country to Culiacán on the west coast of Mexico, where they found other Spaniards.[6] Cabeza de Vaca brought with him a copper bell, which had been given to him somewhere in Texas and which was described as a "hawk bell, thick and large, figured with a face." He was told that this came from somewhere in the north, and, from what he heard from many different Indians, he concluded that there were rich kingdoms in that direction.

After he reached Culiacán, he was sent to Mexico City to tell the Spanish viceroy, Antonio de Mendoza, of his adventure and, particularly, of the rich kingdoms to the north. The wealth of these kingdoms was so fabulous that Cabeza de Vaca was called to Spain to tell the king all about them, too.

Cabeza de Vaca's report added more glitter to the earlier tales of Cortés and Pizarro; he told of an even richer kingdom, known to the Indians as Cibola, or Buffalo Land, which the Spaniards soon called the Seven Silver Cities of Cibola. The Spaniards in America had actually heard of a wealthy kingdom in the north, called Topira, six years before Cabeza de Vaca arrived in Culiacán with his copper bell.[7]

In 1530, an Indian called Tejo, probably from West Texas, told of a visit to a country to the north where there were "seven very large towns which had streets of silver workers." There he had acquired a large amount of gold and silver. When Nuñez de Guzmán, the governor of New Galicia (Northwest Mexico and the unexplored lands beyond), heard this, he organized an expedition of four hundred Spaniards and twenty thousand friendly Indians to look for Topira. The search had to be abandoned, however, because of the rough mountains along the way. Before he could try again, Tejo died.

But the reality of Cabeza de Vaca's little copper bell gave him an audience with the viceroy and the king that set in motion a treasure hunt of massive proportions. In 1538, Guzmán was replaced by Francisco Vásquez de Coronado as governor, with carte blanche to carry on the conquest of whatever the country to the north might be called — Topira, Toyopa, or Cibola. Coronado wrote to the Viceroy Mendoza[8] that he had heard that "the natives [of Topira] wear gold and emeralds and other precious stones. They make general use of gold and silver, with which they cover their houses. The leaders wear finely worked large gold chains around their necks." To find and conquer this ultimate treasure, Coronado organized the biggest treasure hunt the world has ever known.

Earlier legends of treasure go back long before the time when the Spaniards came to America. The ancient myth of a land of paradise was first recorded by Plato in his account of Atlantis. The myth was kept alive by the reports Marco Polo brought back from his travels in Asia from 1271 to 1295. It was encouraged again by the invention of Antilia, a land supposedly on the other side of the world from Europe and beyond China. Antilia was said to be made up of seven islands, each with a city-state, and was far richer than any country Marco Polo had seen. In fact, Columbus was headed for Antilia when he discovered America.

When printing became popular, some two hundred years after Marco Polo's journey, adventure stories set in imaginative lands were the rage. The best seller of 1508 was the *Amadís de Gaula,* published in Zaragoza, Spain, which recorded a good many fantastic tales.[9] Later books were even more imaginative, until they were all capped by the satire of *Don Quixote,* written by Cervantes and first published in 1605.

These stories of adventure and romance were carried to the New World by the earliest European explorers. Cortés was the first to discover that the fantasies were far less spectacular than the real things he found when he conquered Mexico in 1521. In 1533, spurred by the legend of El Dorado (the gilded king), Pizarro went to South America and found wealth beyond his wildest dreams.

With Cabeza de Vaca's account, however, the Kingdom of the Seven Silver Cities became the repository of greater treasures than all those found by Cortés and Pizarro. The biggest treasure hunt the world has ever known was organized to find this fabulous wealth — Coronado's search for the Seven Silver Cities of Cibola and, later, Gran Quivira, which incidentally were the first legends created by the Spaniards of hidden treasure in the Southwest.

It took Coronado four years to get the expedition started. It involved not only himself as governor of New Galicia, but the King of Spain, Emperor Charles V; his viceroy in Mexico, Antonio Mendoza; Marcos de Niza, Franciscan friar, who made the first recorded trip to what is now Arizona; and so many others then living in Mexico that the viceroy checked to find out just how many were involved. Most were going of their own free will. The others, who were not going so willingly, were more or less riff-raff, and the viceroy wasn't sorry to see them go. Maybe they wouldn't come back. Some didn't.

Cabeza de Vaca, perhaps still footsore from hig eight-year journey across the country, stayed home. So did Maldonado and Dorantes, who married widows and settled down in Mexico. Estevan (or Esteban) as an interpreter for the Indian guides who knew the way to Cibola went along with the advance party, led by Fray Marcos de Niza. The Franciscan friar had been sent ahead with instructions to follow near the coast in order to learn what the country was like. However, he decided to delay his investigation of that part of the country until he returned, as he explained in his report to Viceroy Mendoza on September 2, 1539: [10]

> I always tried by all possible means to learn about a country with many settlements and with people more advanced and cultured than those I met in northern Mexico . . . . I sent Esteban de Dorantes, a Negro, whom I instructed to go fifty or sixty leagues toward the north to see whether, by that route, information could be obtained of something important of what we were seeking. I arranged with him that, should he learn of some inhabited and rich country, something really important, he should not go any farther but return in person or send me Indians bearing the following sign we had agreed on: if it were something moderate, he should send me a white cross a span in size (nine inches); if it were of greater importance, he should send me one two spans in size; and if it were something greater and better than New Spain. he should send me a large cross . . . . Four days later messengers from Esteban arrived carrying a very large cross the height of a man.
>
> Later I had received other messengers from him bringing another cross the size of the first one he had sent. He urged me to hurry, affirming that the land I was seeking was the best and greatest that had ever been heard of.

Estevan was so eager to get on with his travels that he left the good priest far to the rear, but he continued to send back glowing accounts of what he found — riches beyond their wildest dreams. The priest interpreted these reports in terms of souls to be saved, but the Negro probably decided that he had never had it so good. It would seem that Estevan knew how to get along with the Indian women as he passed through their villages, and he was well provided with turquoise for trading purposes. Whether his repute as a ladies' man or as a sharp trader brought about his end, no one knows, for the last report of Estevan was of his death. Some accounts say the people of Cibola killed him because he carried a gourd that had been given to him by their enemies.

Fray Marcos de Niza only had a glimpse of one of the Pueblo Indian villages, which he hoped to be a part of something greater and better than anything yet found in Mexico. But encouraged by his account of it, Coronado went ahead with his preparations to capture the Seven Silver Cities of Cibola.

This greatest of all treasure hunts actually went on for years and covered much of Northwest Mexico and the unexplored country beyond. From 1520 when Cortés conquered Mexico, until Coronado returned from his epic search in 1541, it is a history of that period. It has frequently been described as an adventure and as a conquest, which it was. But above all, it was a treasure hunt that continues to the present — without the enormous organization, but with as great fervor.

I often heard in my travels of the search of the Seven Silver Cities. It is the only legend I heard of that seems to have been known throughout the entire Southwest. Sometimes people argued over the exact route Coronado had followed. More often they conjectured as to the real location of the Seven Cities and their wealth, which Coronado had failed to find.

Briefly, here is the story of the Coronado expedition according to the many accounts that have been written about it by those who took part.[11]

After a journey of six weeks and five hundred miles or more that brought near starvation to all, Coronado captured the first of the Seven Silver Cities of Cibola — the Zuni Indian town known as Hawikuh. To his chagrin, the fabled cities were only houses made of mud. Except for a few bits of turquoise, there was no wealth at all.

In spite of his disappointment, he hadn't given up. He settled with his army on the Rio Grande and wrote to the Viceroy Mendoza on August 3, 1540: [12]

> As far as I can judge, it does not appear to me that there is any hope of getting gold or silver [in Cibola] but I trust in God, if there is any, we shall get our share of it and it shall not escape us through any lack of diligence in the search.

His captains were sent to explore the country, discovering the Hopi Indian villages and the Grand Canyon to the northwest. To the east, beyond the Pecos River, they saw the Great Plains and learned of the buffalo. They lost their interest in buffalo after they had met an early West Texan, whom they called The Turk, because he looked like one. This Indian told them so much about the wealth of gold and silver in a country he could lead them to, that the Spaniards returned posthaste to Coronado.

The Turk — who may have told some tall tales such as Texans are reputed to indulge in, even today — had no trouble holding Coronado's interest. From what he heard, Coronado created a legend of his own — the Kingdom of Quivira. It was even greater than the Seven Silver Cities, bigger and richer. His entire army would be needed to find and conquer it. As it marched across the plains of the Texas Panhandle, the army must have been an impressive sight to Indians met on the way.

First there was Coronado, glitteringly arrayed in a suit of gilded armor, with a fine helmet ornamented with plumes. He was followed by "one thousand horses, five hundred [of our] cattle, more than five thousand rams and sheep, and more than fifteen hundred persons, including allies

"THE KINGDOM OF THE SEVEN SILVER CITIES." Storied rock houses, like these in the Mesa Verde National Park, were built by the Pueblo Indians long before the Spaniards came to America. These so impressed the desert Indians to the south that they described them to the Spaniards as being the biggest and finest cities they had ever seen — which they were, when compared with their own settlements of brush-covered huts.

When the Spaniards heard of the Indian accounts of the inhabitants to the north, they embellished them with lavish hoards of silver and gold to conform with the legends they had brought with them to the New World.

CORONADO CROSSED THE BLACK RIVER by ferry along the same trail his Indian guides had been using for generations as they went back and forth between northern Mexico and the Pueblo Indian towns — Cibola.

The trail followed the only direct route by which horsemen, and later wagons, could travel. It led north from the Indian settlements west of the Sierra Madre of Mexico, following and crossing water courses; it climbed plateaus and went on, through the only passage free of lava beds. It wound up and down the canyon walls of the Black River, called the Rafts because the Spaniards "had to cross on these, at it was rising."

Later the route that Coronado followed became a trail used by the U.S. Army, first for cavalry and then for wagon trains, from Fort Wingate, Arizona, to Forts Grant and Bowie and Camp Crittenden. Cattlemen used it to drive their roundups to market.

The route followed by Coronado and his hundred soldiers — seventy-five mounted — along with many Indian allies, was described in such detail by Castañeda, who made the journey with them, that it may be spotted on the ground. And when seen from the air, it is the only route that could have been taken by horsemen over the escarpment of the Gila Mountains, through the lava beds of Ash Flat, and across the gorge of Black River.

When Coronado returned from his search for Cibola and Quivira, he followed an easier but more roundabout route by way of the Rio Grande. This became the trail from Santa Fe to Chihuahua City and on to the rest of Mexico.

and servants." Still " . . . they left no more traces when they got through than if no one had passed. . . ."

So wrote Castañeda, Coronado's historian.[13] Yet volumes have since been written to prove where Coronado's trail passed. It must have been spread at least five hundred miles wide to have touched all the places where claims for its location have since been made.

After wandering on the plains for more than a month and finding only buffalo-hunting Indians who said that Quivira lay to the north, Coronado became suspicious of his guide, The Turk. When he confessed that he had only wanted the Spaniards to provide him protection on his way home, he was put under guard and later strangled "so that he never woke up," according to Castañeda.

But in spite of the information from the Plains Indians and the advice of his officers, Coronado was determined to go on. The main army was sent back to the Rio Grande and, with only thirty horsemen and a new guide, Coronado now turned to the north, determined that he would find the Kingdom of Quivira. After marching another month, he did.

Gran Quivira — Coronado's own legendary kingdom that was richer than the Seven Silver Cities of Cibola — turned out to be only a land of straw and mud villages, the inhabitants barely covered with buffalo skins!

After all the hardships suffered by the expedition, Spaniard and Indian alike, to say nothing of the actual cost to the king and the Mexican viceroy, did any of them ever ask what had started the search for the Seven Cities in the first place? The only *real* thing was a copper bell given to Cabeza de Vaca somewhere in West Texas, which probably came from Mexico anyway.

However, Castañeda summed it up neatly when he wrote: [14] "Granted that they did not find the riches of which they had been told, they found a place in which to search for them."

And the search goes on. Not only for the Seven Silver Cities of Cibola and Gran Quivira but for all the other legendary wealth that abounds in the Southwest since Coronado set out four hundred years ago.

There are hundreds of legends of all sorts. You can pick the one you like best. If you live long enough in the Southwest, with its rugged mountains, deserts, plains, and pine forests, its ruins of Indian dwellings, Spanish missions, and frontier forts, you might even have a legend of your own, as did Coronado with his Gran Quivira, Sergeant Jones with his Treasure, Rod with his Pots of Gold, and I with the Lost Mountain of Uranium.

Legends of buried treasures and lost mines in the Southwest were started by the Spanish conquistadores, kept alive by their descendants, and later, by the first Anglo settlers. Generations of these pioneers have seen the country grow to what it is today, but the old legends never die, and new ones have been added.

Many who have sought wealth in the Southwest have found it — not by looking for legendary riches but by ranching, farming, mining, trading, and banking. Others have found their fortunes in the fruits of their creative imagination.

But what is it about the Southwest that is so conducive to visions of riches?

TREASURE-HUNTING CAN BE SERIOUS BUSINESS. Ted DeGrazia, Tucson artist, and fellow adventurers return from the Catalina Mountains where the Mine with the Iron Door[15] and other legendary treasures await the finder. Not content with just painting, illustrating, and creating textile designs, jewelry, and ceramics, DeGrazia is also a collector of myths and legends, an historian of the Southwest, and a writer of archaeological fantasies.

Region of Riches

WHAT IS THIS COUNTRY LIKE, which the Spanish and others who have followed them have found so irresistibly fertile a place for visions? And what sort of places hold legends of buried treasures and lost mines?

The Southwest reaches from the Gulf of Mexico to the Pacific Ocean; from the plains and mountains in the north to the deserts extending far south into Mexico. It includes all that part of the American continent claimed by the Spanish explorers which lies west of the Mississippi River. For the most part, it is outside the regions where Cortés and Pizarro gathered their fabulous loot so readily.

The Southwest has long been a rich mining country — with gold, silver, and copper deposits. The accounts of these provided more than enough incentive to look for more. The country is huge, and there are hundreds of legends of treasures and lost mines. The kinds of places where the legendary wealth is hidden can be pointed out.

They are everywhere. Along the coasts of the Pacific Ocean and the Gulfs of California and Mexico are wrecks of ships, waiting to be found. Every river, from where it empties into the sea to where it starts winding its way past rocky cliffs, provides hiding places for undiscovered legendary riches.

But the greatest wealth, according to legends, is concealed in the mountains. They are the hiding places of all sorts of lost and buried treasures and are usually the locations of the actual mines that produced great wealth. Some of the legends tell of mines hidden by rocks covering their tunnels and their dumps of rich ore. The fact that they have not been found is proof to those who search for them that they must still be somewhere.

Even the forests outside the mountainous regions are places where legendary treasures lie hidden, usually beside some gnarled ancient tree, yet to be identified.

Not to be overlooked are the deserts. Drifting sand and dry river beds, filled with boulders, hide lost treasures. There are outcrops of pure gold and silver waiting to be discovered.

There are legends of treasure everywhere. And they have been created from all sorts of things.

THE OLD JIM BEAM RANCH HOUSE west of the Pecos River where we were caught during a March blizzard that covered the ground with sleet. A cowboy called High Tower shared our refuge.

The wind blew the sharp sleet through the board walls and up through the floor. We put up our tent in one of the rooms, lighted our gasoline cooking stove, and let it burn until the fuel was gone. Then we tore loose planks from the barn and fed them into the little flat-topped stove where we melted ice for coffee water. Most of the days and nights we spent in our bedrolls, fully dressed and shivering.

High Tower told us legend after legend of buried treasures and lost mines of the Big Bend Country. When he ran out of stories, though the blizzard held on, he rode horseback sixty miles into the nearest town.

THE LITTLE WHITEWASHED HOUSE dates from the Spanish settlement along the Rio Grande in Texas.

We spent a cold winter night there at the invitation of the owner because, when we tried to stay outside, the livestock chewed our bedding. A thin blanket, hanging from a wire stretched from wall to wall, separated our sleeping space from that of the family. The father and three older children, wrapped in blankets, slept on the dirt floor with a mat (*petate*) made of river reeds as a mattress. The mother and youngest child occupied the only bed.

Throughout the night I was awakened by the cries of the youngster demanding to be nursed by its mother. The next morning he was scrounging with the older ones for the cigarette butts that had been thrown on the ground during the night, and was smoking along with the others.

A CAVE AT NORIEGA, southeast of Chihuahua City, in the Llano de los Gigantes — Plain of the Giants — where the "rocks are black from much smoke, and many baskets and mats and pots are on the dirt floor," according to our guide. He had seen it many times with a friend.

When we arrived at the cave, we found that his friend's son had moved into it with store-bought furniture and a cook-stove, and had set up housekeeping.

"How long have you lived here?" we asked.

"Many years, señor, since I married."

I looked at his grown daughter standing by her mother and realized that it had been a long time since the cave had been as the old guide described it. Once it must have been filled with deep trash, since pieces of fiber sandals and baskets still were to be found in the dump outside the wall that had been built across the shelter.

All I learned from the trip was that time means little to these people, who tell of boyhood experiences as though they had happened yesterday.

My guide and the son of his old friend talked together long into the night about the buried treasures that might still be hidden in the cave.

"THERE'S A LITTLE HOUSE at the end of a dim road. They can tell you."
This was often the answer when we asked how to get to some particular
place. And when we did reach the house, they did guide us, some times
by way of a dimmer road, sometimes by following wagon tracks.

More often than not, someone was glad to go along to show the way
and to tell of the legends of buried treasure they were sure we must really
be looking for rather than the old ruins we had asked about.

OUR CAMP IN THE BARRANCA COUNTRY of the Sierra Madre of Chihuahua. Young Gus McGinnis, son of the foreman of the Hearst Ranch at Las Varas, Chihuahua, was our guide and looked after the pack mules and riding horses. He knew the way only for the first twenty miles. Then we picked up another guide for the next ten miles and a third guide for the rest of the way.

A two-weeks trip had been planned into the deep canyons of the rough country. There we found the old cliff dwellings, the object of our archaeological work. It seemed as though the owners had abandoned the ruins as they heard us coming up the steep ledges and had not managed to take all their possessions with them.

In camp our guides talked among themselves of the Toyopa treasures somewhere on beyond.

"When the priests left, they buried the treasure under the church and tore it down . . ."

"They say the bells still ring on a windy night . . ."

At the end of a week, I was well along with my work when young Gus told me we would soon have to leave.

"Why?" I asked. "We came to spend two weeks!"

"We have little to eat."

"But we brought three pack mules — mostly grub — and corn for them!" And I pointed to a pack still hardly touched, filled with ham and bacon and cans of preserved fruits and vegetables we had brought from the Mormon settlements at Casas Grandes. "What about that?"

"But there's no corn, not even for the mules."

"How come?"

"Made tortillas of it. Now we have only beans and coffee."

There was nothing to do but pack up and leave — only the food one knows, satisfies!

JESUIT GOLD has attracted so many treasure-hunting diggers that walls start falling into holes in the ground as at this ruin in northwestern Chihuahua.

Legends tell that when the Jesuit priests were driven out of the country in 1767, they hid all their gold and silver and never had a chance to come back and get it.

Yet the records of the Jesuit Order show that their priests were prohibited from mining by their own rules and by Spanish law. Only two instances are known in which the priests were involved in mining operations in the Sierra Madre of northern Mexico and both times those involved were severely reprimanded and removed.

Jesuit records contain no reference to any concealed wealth or lost missions. Church decorations, sometimes rich in paintings, gilded carvings, and silver communion plate, came from the headquarters of the religious orders in Mexico City or regional centers such as Guadalajara. Seldom were they as rich as treasure hunters would have them, nor were the decorations made locally.

But " . . . the Padres could often claim quite justly that their frontier churches were equal to many a cathedral in Europe," Father Charles W. Polzer, S.J., wrote in the *Desert Magazine* in August, 1962: "No doubt precious relics of the mission era remain undiscovered."[16]

And so the search goes on! And on!

A PLACE TO LOOK FOR HIDDEN TREASURE. This large rock shelter in Chihuahua, not far from Monteseco on the Rio Conchos, was occupied during prehistoric times, but most of the old rubbish was cleared out recently when the low stone walls were built. These walls had provided shelter for the families of the Mexican workmen who were cutting mescal that grew on the mountainside. The plants were carried by burros to the Rio Conchos in the valley below where they were roasted in earthen pits like those used in prehistoric times, and then were distilled for alcoholic drinks.

While I salvaged what I could, my guide was busy looking for treasure hidden where the Mexican workers had recently lived.

"Why look there?" I asked. "They left nothing but the ashes from their fires."

"Well," he explained, pushing over a wall of loosely laid rocks, "if they found treasure, they had to hide it. Maybe they have had no time to come back and carry it away."

If there is no legend of buried treasure, one will surely be created to account for the digging that has been done by others in places where treasure *could* be hidden!

TUMBLED STONE WALLS are the only remains of this old way-station on the Butterfield Stage Route twenty miles south of Abilene.

The Butterfield Trail, also called the Southern Overland or Emigrant Route, was the longest in miles but the shortest in terms of years of use, of any of the old routes in the Southwest. It went from St. Louis to San Francisco, a distance of 2,800 miles, and was used only from 1858 until 1861 at the outbreak of the Civil War.

Stages then traveled the route of the Pony Express from St. Joseph, Missouri, to San Francisco by way of Salt Lake City. This route continued to be used until the railroads replaced the stagecoaches, beginning in 1869.

The Santa Fe Trail went south from Santa Fe to Mexico by way of El Paso, following the route Coronado had used on his return from Cibola and Gran Quivira. Later, overland travel from the east went to Mexico from Independence, Missouri, by way of Santa Fe or by way of San Antonio on the Chihuahua Trail that passed through El Paso.

There were other trails too that connected the cities in Mexico with the settlements in California, Arizona, New Mexico and Texas. But no matter where the old routes went or how well they might have been guarded with forts and way-stations, the travelers who used them were always threatened by robbery. The legends of loot taken and hidden, and still being looked for, would add up to a large part of all the gold and silver the country ever produced.

THE SECRET SOCIETY of some prehistoric Indian tribe might have met in the little rock shelter shown here beside the man. There were deeply incised and rubbed grooves on the sandstone walls, different from the simple grooves used in the sharpening of bone and wooden implements. The old campfires and stone tools along the banks of Oak Creek told the story of people being there long before Fort Chadburn, Texas, the old frontier post, was built close by.

It was during Prohibition, in 1928, when I asked permission of the owner of the land (on which the old stone buildings still stood) to excavate the little cave. He looked me over with a scowl on his sunburned face and shook his head. But his scowl was replaced with a grin when I told him, "I'll stay away from your pigs — I smelled them a quarter of a mile away!"

"Okay," he nodded. He knew I had smelled the sour mash that came from a bootleg-still hidden nearby.

"And I could use a little well-cured pork," I suggested. "About five gallons."

"Come by when you get ready to go," he said, "and I'll fix you up."

The petroglyphs I uncovered, shown here in part, were unlike any I had ever seen. What they might have meant, if they were made to record or convey some meaning, may never be known.

Some treasure hunter must have seen the petroglyphs after my visit and interpreted the signs to be a map, the crosses and arrows indicating the spot where treasure lay, for years later, I learned that the shelter had been completely destroyed by dynamiting.

IS THE TRAIL to the lost Adams Diggings marked by this twisted tree trunk? This alligator-bark juniper in the Fort Apache Indian Reservation grows within the country where one of the greatest of all lost mines, according to legend, was first found. The Adams Diggings have since been sought over a large part of northeastern Arizona and adjoining regions. Is the guide to its location marked by the twisted trunk of the old tree, perhaps bent as a sapling to mark an Indian trail?

It all started in 1864, with a freighter known only as Adams. He had lost his wagons and all but twelve of his horses, his saddle, and his gun, in an Indian raid near Yuma, Arizona. Soon afterwards, Adams joined twelve prospectors who had just learned from a young Mexican, called Gotch Ear, of gold that could be picked up like gravel. Gotch Ear had lived with the Apache Indians. He had fled because he had killed one of them, the murderer of Gotch Ear's brother.

Gotch Ear wanted a saddle horse so that he might return to Mexico, and the others wanted to know how to find the gold. According to the late J. Frank Dobie,[17] he "finally consented to act as guide" in exchange for "two horses, a saddle, a gun, ammunition, two fifty dollar gold pieces, and a red silk bandana." All this was to be his after he had shown where the gold was.

For days the party traveled to the northeast, crossing a dim wagon trail that Gotch Ear said led to Fort Wingate, and passing a pile of rocks with three sticks on it to tell that three Apache Indians had gone that way and would return.

Soon Gotch Ear led them to the spot by way of a rough canyon in which the gold-filled stream ran. It was even richer than they had dreamed. Only some of it was ever carried away. The Apaches returned and only three of the white men escaped — a German, Adams, and a prospector by the name of Davidson. But they carried with them a tale of gold that has spread through a large part of the Southwest. The trail that leads to the mouth of the canyon is still sought.

THE SUPERSTITION MOUNTAINS hide within themselves more than twenty lost mines according to legends. It all started in 1846 after the Peraltas, wealthy Spanish landowners of Mexico, "took fabulous amounts of gold out from a mine until the Apache Indians rose up and massacred the party," according to Randolph Riley, U.S. forest ranger in the Superstition Mountains.[18]

The most famous of all the lost mines in the Superstitions is the Lost Dutchman, which was reported in about 1864 by Jacob Walz. According to his story, he had found the old Peralta lode, which produced a fortune. Riley is quoted as saying that the Lost Dutchman Mine could only be ore high-graded "from another mine and hid" in the Superstitions. Walz is known to have worked as a miner in the Wickenburg diggings, which did produce gold.

According to Riley, the Superstitions are said to have claimed the lives of more than thirty men disputing over searchers' rights.

In 1962, Miss Celeste Marie Jones, a former opera singer, laid claim to searchers' rights which others disputed in spite of the armed camp that she had set up.

One of her followers, Robert St. Marie, was killed by Ed Piper, a rival gold-seeker, in self-defense, according to the *Tucson Daily Citizen,* June 2, 1962, which reported: "Plagued by recurring flareups between the rival parties, Pinal County officers moved in after the shooting and took rifles away from the two camps, but left them their side arms."

So famous has the Lost Dutchman Mine become that the Dons Club of Phoenix provides a tour for those "who thrill to the adventures and beauties of the wilderness." They advertise a guided trip "into the mysterious Superstition Mountains to renew the search for the legendary 'Lost Dutchman Mine.'"

THE OLD SAN SABA PRESIDIO northwest of San Antonio was said to have been the hiding place of James Bowie (the famous Texan who died defending the Alamo) while he was looking for gold and silver he had heard about from his Apache friends in 1831. According to legend, the presidio was built by the Spaniards as protection for the miners working nearby. But Bowie was years too late; others had been looking for the same rich mines beginning with Don Bernardo de Miranda, Lieutenant General of the Province of Texas, who had been ordered to investigate the mining possibilities in February, 1756! His reports were so glowing that the hunt was on — and still is going strong today — for Los Almagres, Las Amarillas, La Mina de las Iguanas, the San Saba, the Lost Bowie, and all the other fabulously rich mines of gold and silver that legends tell of. The last time I saw the old presidio, the walls were falling into the holes dug on all sides by treasure hunters, but the ruin has since been restored and is now a Texas state park.

A STREAM OF GOLD AND SILVER has passed over the Rio Grande where it marks the Texas-Mexico boundary. The flow of tales of treasure that has crossed it since the Spaniards first saw it four hundred years ago is mightier than the river itself. Legends tell of treasures of coins, in leather bags and chests of wood and iron, scattered from the piney woods of east Texas to the high plains.

This stream of wealth, which began to flow into the Southwest with the first Spanish settlers following Coronado's entry in 1539 continued during the Mexican sovereignty and even into recent times. [19]

Spanish and Mexican troops must have been disappointed on more than one payday, according to tales of payrolls that were lost on their way from Mexico. Some people still search for the treasures hidden by General Santa Ana's army during the War of Texas Independence. Robbers account for other troves. Much of it was brought from the south by wealthy refugees escaping the frequent Mexican revolutions. American merchants sent goods into Mexico along the Santa Fe and Chihuahua trails, by way of El Paso; others sent them through San Antonio.

All roads crossed the Rio Grande, and the search still goes on for the legendary treasures lost and hidden along the way.

THE OLD COPPER KING MINE in the Twin Buttes District, twenty miles south of Tucson, was once a rich lode of surface ore worked by hand. It may have been the source of the copper that was milled at Tumacacori, the Spanish mission built in 1772, only twenty miles farther south.

Later, shafts were sunk by Arizona miners, and ores, not so rich as those at the surface, were removed by the use of machinery. Recently, the whole area has been found to contain a large, deep body of low-grade copper ore that can be worked profitably only after millions of dollars have been spent in development.

Rich gold and silver mines worked by the Spaniards in the Southwest were described in the *Rudo Ensayo,* by an anonymous traveler of 1762, who gave a first-hand account of the country that is now southern Arizona and northern Sonora. A hundred years later, many of the same locations were again mentioned by J. Ross Browne, whose travels through Arizona in 1864 furnished a full picture of the country. But at that time, few of the old mines were still being worked.

Today, only the large deposits of low-grade ores are being mined profitably; most of them are open pits that have long ago swallowed the places where the earlier rich ores had been discovered and worked by hand. But the legendary lost mines are still being hunted.

OLD BUILDINGS AT FORT MCKAVETT, TEXAS, on the San Saba River, one hundred and twenty-five miles northwest of San Antonio is a likely place to dig for treasures, according to legends. The old Chihuahua City Trail, by way of El Paśo, passed this way. Here was the frontier when the Spaniards settled in Texas. It was still the frontier in 1852 when Fort McKavett and others were built to protect settlers living to the east. Later the line of frontier forts had moved only a hundred miles to the west, and there the frontier remained until the 1880's, when the railroads replaced the stage lines, the buffalo had been slaughtered and the Indians rounded up and held on their reservations. Legendary loot from Indian raids and from other robberies still lies hidden somewhere. Any ruin is a likely place to look.

A STORMY SEA has wrecked many treasure-laden ships on some rocky shore. The recovery of wreckage from ships of yesterday carrying precious metals and gems — the only kind of cargo that could survive through the years — is the finding of lost treasures. The recent accounts[20] in magazines and newspapers of the salvage of gold and silver coins and bullion, with ship wreckage, off the shore of Fort Pierce, Florida, will spur the search for other wrecked cargoes. And even greater efforts will be made to locate the legendary ones.

Many legends have grown out of the ships that sailed the Gulf of Mexico into the Atlantic as well as the Pacific, since America's discovery by Europeans. Chinese porcelains and silks were brought to America by way of the Pacific Ocean and often transshipped to Europe, after being packed on mule back and by ox cart across Mexico. Through the Gulf of Mexico and across the Atlantic sailed the treasure-laden ships of the Spanish explorers and later, as the rich mines were worked, the ships filled with silver and gold bullion. The ships that returned to America brought all the things the new country required.

Pirates soon preyed on the eastbound ships and brigands smuggled into America the things the mother countries forbade the colonies to make for themselves. Often these smuggled goods had been stolen from the westbound ships.

Jean Lafitte, probably the best known and most successful pirate and brigand, dominated the Gulf of Mexico during his time. The treasures he is known to have stolen, and legends say are still buried, have been hunted for more than a hundred years. And the search is intensified each time any kind of ancient shipwreck is recovered from off any shore in America.

THE SILVER CITY of Alamos, a Spanish colonial town in Sonora, Mexico, was the center of the richest mining district in the world in 1750. Its mining history starts in 1683 with the miraculous appearance of a beautiful maiden standing on top of a great cactus, which led to the discovery of silver nearby.[21] From then until 1850, Alamos was a city that thrived on silver. Alamos began as an Indian village — the Place of the Cottonwood Trees — before the Spaniards came to America. Cabeza de Vaca must have passed that way as Coronado did later. Father Kino, the Franciscan priest, must have gone near it when he first began building missions that led to the settlement of Sonora and Arizona. The Camino Real passed through Alamos.

During Alamos' prosperity, the inhabitants carried on industry and trade and built the public and private buildings said to be some of the finest examples of Spanish Colonial architecture in Mexico. The years that followed this period of glory in Alamos witnessed the struggles of the country to survive in the face of Indian trouble which threatened from early times, revolutions, wars between the United States and later France — as well as floods and droughts.

Alamos is now the home of many Americans from the United States who have found it a refuge into the past, and of the Mexicans, many of whom are the direct descendants of those who built Alamos and can tell of the former riches. Some of these riches still exist in the legends of the treasures buried in the hills by the wealthy mine owners when they were faced with some of the many disasters that finally forced them to give up.

A SPANISH SMELTER is the explanation frequently given this old lime kiln, dug into the red clay (Permian) bank of the Clear Fork of the Brazos River, north of Abilene. The hot fires that once burned in the jug-like hole — more than six feet across and eight feet deep — had made the lining of the pit as hard as brick. Slag from burned limestone gave the appearance of a small but active mining operation abandoned long ago. Only the gold and silver that legend provides were absent. In their place were the rich copper nodules "like potatoes" often found in that part of Texas in the Permian beds. The nodules have been identified by some Texas geologists as coprolites — the petrified dung of reptiles, ancestors of the dinosaurs. In the beds are also pseudomorphs in the form of logs of wood that "may at one time have been wood, but now has been transformed into copper." There are many fossil remains of vertebrate animals and reptilian teeth.[22]

These copper ores were first discovered by Captain Randolph B. Marcy in 1852 while exploring the Red River.[23] Since 1864, many attempts have been made to mine these copper ores, and, like the old lime kiln, the relics of these operations have now become a part of the legendary treasures of that section of Texas.

The kiln must have supplied some of the lime used by the builders of nearby Fort Phantom Hill in 1851. The old oak logs in the fort had been chinked with lime. Lime was also used for mortar in the stone chimneys which stood long after the log buildings had been burned when the fort was abandoned in 1854.

Spanish smelters, according to legends, are within fifty miles of where the Salt and Double Mountain forks join the Brazos River — the site of one of the richest hoards of Spanish treasure in that part of Texas.

THE SPANISH TREASURE of the Brazos River, according to legends, lies hidden somewhere within fifty miles of this spot, where the Double Mountain and Salt forks join the Brazos River of Texas. When I first heard of the Spanish treasure, it consisted of a hoard of gold and silver left by the Spaniards when they were driven out by the Indians in the 1700's and had to abandon their rich mines. How much greater the treasure has grown in the past fifty years is shown by an account in *Argosy Magazine* in May, 1965.[24]

This account states that the main treasure has not yet been found, although there is a map, still uncoded, showing its location. The account also tells of the finding of silver statuettes, crosses, nuggets, diamond necklaces, gold buttons, Spanish armor, and enough other relics to fill a small museum. There are clues to be followed in the Indian camps, the ruins of Spanish smelters, missions, mines, graves with skeletons — even mastodon teeth and bones and scores of "plat" rocks with uncoded messages scratched on their surfaces. There are so many clues they must be piled on top of one another!

In 1934, I excavated in the Pleistocene deposits, which lie near the surface at the forks of the Brazos River. This area has long been known to scientists as rich in fossil bones. I was looking for ancient man and found the bones of mammoth, giant tortoise, and great long-horned bison. Along with them was charcoal that might have come from the cooking fires of elephant hunters whose kill-sites (places where the bones of elephants and the stone implements of their hunters had been found) were then being uncovered on the plains. The fires of pre-Spanish inhabitants must have burned during many centuries in the old camp sites that dot the high bluffs overlooking the Brazos for miles.

Within a radius of fifty miles, archaeology records more than ten thousand years of history as told by the stone weapons of the first hunters; in burials, hearthstones, and strange signs painted and pecked on rocks; and, last of all, in glass beads and metal arrowheads. These first came to the Indians from the French (and later from the Spaniards) who also provided them with firearms and horses and all the other things that gave the Indians a new way of life long before the white man settled all of the Southwest.

All of these things — like the old lime kiln and the remains of attempts to mine the copper in the Permian red beds — are now clues to the Spanish Treasure of the Brazos. I sometimes wonder if my digging there has now become another tale of fruitless search for this legendary gold and silver.

ANCIENT SHIPS LIE BURIED beneath the desert sands somewhere between the Colorado River and the San Bernardino Mountains of California, according to legends. Within this region is the Basin of the Salton Sea, a remnant of the Gulf of California when it reached far to the north.

Who sailed these ancient ships? Those who seek the treasures they are said to have carried give a number of answers: some say the Phoenicians; others, the Vikings; and still others, the Spaniards.

Treasures or Trivia?

DURING THE EIGHTEEN YEARS I was curator of the Arizona State Museum I again heard of many of the peculiar things connected with legends that I had first heard while working as an archaeologist.

In my talks with thousands of our visitors, some told me of the legends they had known, and they frequently asked about old maps showing where treasures or lost mines are to be found (the museum has none).

Often our visitors asked about — and sometimes brought with them — peculiar things that museums are supposed to be able to explain. Some of these were considered to be "clues" to legendary treasure. Usually these turned out to be archaeological remains of some sort such as burials, rock circles, house walls, mortar holes (for grinding), and other indications of early inhabitants. Most of these inhabitants were as lacking in wealth as were the people found by Coronado. The historical ruins such as ghost towns, old army posts, Spanish missions, and abandoned ranch houses — all considered by treasure hunters as promising places to look — were just as bare of anything that could be called treasures. History says that these early inhabitants of the Southwest had little use for money as their wants were filled by their own efforts or by trading.

Other "clues" sometimes included an isolated boulder different from nearby rock formations, or trees growing in an odd manner, a landscape that was peculiar-looking when viewed from a single spot, the way clouds hung over the mountains, or reflections in still water.

The Southwest — rich in archaeological ruins, the history of exploration and conquest, living Indian customs, a variety of landscape unequaled in the rest of the country, a mining and frontier spirit — is filled with the sort of things that serve as clues to hidden treasure and lost mines. Most frequent of all are the signs often identified with those used by prehistoric Indians as well as by the living ones.

As interpreted by treasure hunters, signs were used by those who hid mythical wealth in order to lead the seeker astray. How far one can be led astray is shown by some of the peculiar things that I learned about as archaeologist and curator of the museum.

This account of the ramifications that follow the interpretation of Indian signs may seem even a greater digression than often occurs in the accounts given by some seekers of legendary wealth. But this is the record . . .

77

Signs, Symbols, and Saints

A MUSEUM VISITOR gave me a slip of paper with signs on it like these:

As I looked them over, I thought, "What are they?" He explained: "They're Indian signs that tell where to look for treasure."

I tried to recall some of the legends I had heard of Indians who had hidden their gold and silver from the white man but had left signs to show the locations.

"They do use these signs, don't they?" the visitor asked.

"They could," I admitted, and suggested that we see what signs could be found in the museum collections — blankets, baskets, pottery and other artifacts.

We found that the reproductions of the Navajo sand paintings, such as those shown below, contained many designs that have definite meaning to the Navajos:

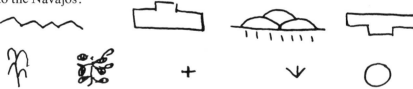

The only designs that had any similarity to those brought in by the visitor were some on pottery, used by the ancient Hohokam, the prehistoric desert dwellers of Arizona. Resemblances might be claimed in their use of a variety of X's, as well as in other designs that could be compared to letters of the alphabet.

I felt that my visitor was satisfied that we hadn't found much to compare with his signs, but he hadn't given up.

"How about Indian writings on rocks?" he asked.

I mentioned several books that had been published with full description and illustrations of pictographs and petroglyphs.

"Any close to Tucson that I could see?"

A PICTURE STORY. This pictograph showing three hunters with bows and arrows, stalking two buffalo and two mountain lions, was painted on rocks at the Hueco Tanks, an archaeological site northeast of El Paso.

The scene is realistic and represents the sort of thing with which a prehistoric artist could have been familiar. But does it show a hunt that took place or a wish for a successful one? Or a scene in which the hunters and the animals are expressions of some abstract idea? Only the artist could explain.

If the signs are translated according to the guide for finding treasure, they say only that water is to the right. The zig-zag line, or snake, represents water, and there is water to the right — the direction in which all the living things are facing — and a curved line to show the way. But the prehistoric artist made the rock painting long before any legends of hidden treasure and lost mines in the Southwest called for signs to show their locations.

He left after I had told him of all the nearby places where pictographs could be seen. I wondered if he would keep looking for "Indian signs" until he found something similar to those he had shown me. And if he did, would that provide the clue to the treasure he was looking for?

I thought of other visitors who had been concerned with the meaning of Indian signs. The only answer I could give them was this: There may be as many meanings as there are answers to the questions that museums are often asked, "What is the Indian word for cradle board?" Since there are, or were, a thousand or more Indian languages in America, the word for cradle board could only be the word used by a particular tribe. There is no common language used by all Indians.

In much the same way, Indian signs mean only what their maker intended them to mean. In America, only the higher civilizations, represented by the Maya and Aztec cultures, had a written language. These had developed to the stage in which both pictures and symbols were used to express ideas. An alphabet, with signs to represent sounds, had not been developed — although an efficient system of numerals had been invented. Only some parts of these written records can now be read. The Maya codices are written in a lost language. Until the key is found, only the numerals and the calendar system can be understood, and certain details of even this latter system are in dispute.

Sometimes someone claims to have found a key that opens up the meaning of signs but that works only for the one who has found it.

SYMBOLS

JAMES CHURCHWARD, the creator of the imaginary Continent of Mu, which he located in the Pacific Ocean and which was supposed to have antedated ancient Atlantis, has told how he learned to read symbols that had universal meaning. According to his account in *The Lost Continent of Mu,* he acquired this knowledge in "certain monasteries in India and Tibet whose names are withheld by request" and from a "high priest in a college temple" who was "exceedingly interested in the records of archaeology and the records of the ancients and had a greater knowledge of those subjects than any other living man."[25]

Churchward not only created a universal symbolic language, which he said originated in Mu and spread throughout the world, but he invented keys for the interpretation of pictographs and other signs, wherever they occurred. His interpretations of Southwestern pictographs, signs, and symbols, furnish a history of the country more fantastic than any science-fiction writer could ever provide.

In brief, here is the story which Churchward tells us he deciphered from pictographs:[26] The first settlements were made in the Southwest before the mountains were raised. It is quite apparent that the settlers from Mu, after reaching the mouth of the Colorado River, their objective point from the Motherland, proceeded to work up the river and inland. This took place, Churchward says, some 50,000 years ago.

A somewhat similar interpretation of some Arizona petroglyphs made by the late William Coxon and described by him in the September 1964, *Arizona Highways* magazine, titled "Ancient Manuscripts on American Stones" was reported by Roscoe Willson in his article, "Arizona Rock Pictures Need a Rosetta Stone," in *Arizona Days and Ways Magazine,* January 31, 1965, pp. 26–27: [27] "Coxon was imbued with the idea that some of these figures (petroglyphs) might have been a part of an attempt at a written language;" he claimed that the "so-called geometric figures found in the Old World, and even on scattered islands, for which he found duplicate rock carving in Arizona, had some special worldwide significance" and "should more properly be given the high sounding name 'Cognate-Geometric-Rock-writings'."

The same sorts of pictographs have also been interpreted by others as clues to Spanish treasure and lost mines, hidden hundreds of years after the rock drawings had been made!

The reconstruction of the past, whether by the use of written records or by archaeological and other scientific evidence, aided by a lively imagination, is certainly more interesting than any account restricted to dry facts. Science-fiction of the most fantastic sort, if plausible, can be even more intriguing. But the meaning of Indian signs and designs used in pictographs, sand paintings, and other handicrafts cannot be interpreted unless we know what was intended. They do not give clues to buried treasures and lost mines, nor are they written records of the early history of America. Limited archaeological interpretations can be made of some of them, along with the use of other evidence, to reconstruct this history.

In the Mu books, the factual background of good science-fiction is lacking. Nor can they qualify as good fantasy, such as *Alice in Wonderland* or the *Wizard of Oz,* both completely lacking in plausibility. At best, the Mu books are imaginative creations masquerading as science. However, their popularity is attested to by the many printings of *The Lost Continent of Mu* since its publication in 1931. They must have contributed considerably to the idea that most signs and symbols have universal meanings and all we need to understand them is the proper key.

Only music and some of the sciences — mathematics, astronomy, chemistry — use signs that may be called universal. (Probably the dollar sign ["$"] is also becoming a symbol universally recognized!) Without knowledge of the intention of the maker, nobody can understand the meaning of the Indian signs. Nobody, that is, except someone with supernatural help . . . such as Joseph Smith, prophet and founder of the Mormon Church, is said to have received.

SAINTS

MY FIRST-HAND KNOWLEDGE OF, and contact with, the Mormons began in the early 1930's in Globe at Gila Pueblo.

Some of our frequent visitors were members of the Church of Jesus Christ of Latter-Day Saints from Mesa, sixty miles away. They had settled in the Salt River Valley, east of Phoenix, while Arizona was still a territory, and had built an imposing temple there. Our visitors came seeking answers to many questions of great interest to their sect — as well as to archaeologists the world over. Where did the American Indians come from, they asked, and when? Were the higher American civilizations developed here, or had they been brought in from some outside civilization? And if so, where?

The visitors left copies of the *Book of Mormon* — on which their church was founded — along with piles of religious tracts. From these and later publications, my curiosity led me to learn of the Mormon reconstruction of prehistoric America.

According to the *Book of Mormon,*[28] America was invaded in about 600 B.C., by a small group of Israelites. Warned of the destruction of Jerusalem, they had gone south to the sea, where they built a ship and crossed to America. There they developed a civilization, which later became divided into the Nephites and the Lamanites. They fought, and the Nephites were forced to seek a new homeland.

In about 200 B.C., the Nephites joined with the Mulekites, Israelites who had left Jerusalem in about 587 B.C., and formed a new kingdom under the Nephite ruler, King Mosiah. The new group lived in a part of America where there were ancient ruins of a high civilization. Here twenty-four gold plates were found giving the history of the Jaredites, who had left Jerusalem at about the time the Tower of Babel was built and had come to America in about 2200 B.C. in eight peculiar barges. After about two thousand years they had destroyed themselves with internal wars.

The Mormon account then tells of a long war between the Nephites-Mulekites and the Lamanites, which began in 200 B.C. and was followed by a two-hundred-year peace. During the period of peace, a high civilization was developed with two written languages: one is described as reformed-Egyptian, which is nearest to ancient Phoenician, and the other was a revised Hebrew.

The Nephites were ruled by the Kings Nephi, Benjamin, and Moroni. Mormon, a great Nephite general, compiled the records of his people and abridged the earlier Mulekite record, written on gold plates. Though the Nephites were finally annihilated by the Lamanites in about 420 A.D., Mormon's son, Moroni, survived and hid the records.

This account of the settlement of America is far beyond what archaeologists have discovered, or could ever hope to reconstruct, from archaeological records alone. These records show that Meso-America (parts of Mexico, Central America, and South America), which were identified by the Mormon reconstruction as having been settled by Israelites, was inhabited for two thousand years, more or less, before its European discovery, by various people who had developed the highest prehistoric civilization in America. Some of these cultures, particularly those in Mexico and South America, were still thriving at the time of Spanish conquest. Extensive ruins showed that even greater civilizations — the Mayan — flourished in parts of Central America and Mexico at an earlier date.

Different racial types appear to be represented on certain stone sculptures and wall decorations and, from the style of the clothing, might be compared with Semitic people as the Mormons have claimed in their history. But nothing has been reported in the archaeological record giving specific identity of tribes and the names of rulers as set out in detail in the Mormon accounts.

The historical record of Meso-America does show the widespread myth of a bearded white man who was to return to rule. According to Mormon interpretation, his first appearance was that of Jesus Christ who came to preach in America after His resurrection.

Of more interest to me than the contents of the *Book of Mormon* and the history it gave of prehistoric America, however, are the accounts that have been given of the origin of the book.[29]

Joseph Smith, the fifteen-year-old son of a farmer, living near Palmyra, New York in 1820, said he had had a vision in answer to his prayers for help in deciding which sect of the Christian religion he should follow.

"None!" answered one of the two personages who appeared to him in a pillar of light.[30]

Three years later, on September 21, 1823, Joseph Smith had another vision, in which he was visited by a white-robed, barefoot figure who said his name was Moroni and that he was a messenger of God. Moroni told him, "There was a book deposited, written upon gold plates, giving an account of the former inhabitants of this continent, and the source from which they sprang."

According to *Joseph Smith Tells His Own Story,* prepared and distributed by the Church of Jesus Christ of Latter-Day Saints, Moroni also told him that there were "two stones in silver bows — and these stones, fastened to a breastplate, constituted what is called the Urim and Thummim — deposited with the plates; and the possession and use of these stones were what constituted 'seers' in ancient or former times; and that God had prepared them for the purpose of translating the book."[31]

The vision was repeated three times with the same message, warning that Joseph Smith alone would be held responsible for the gold plates and that he was charged by God to translate and deliver the message they bore.

These revelations so exhausted the young man that he fainted the next day when he attempted to work. Moroni came to him again, repeating the message and telling him to confide in his father. When he did this, his father told him to do as commanded.

Joseph Smith then went to the place where the plates were deposited — Cumorah Hill, near Palmyra, New York — which he had seen in his vision. There he found a stone box, all but covered by earth. After some exertion he managed to remove the lid. Inside he saw all that he had been told of. But three years passed before he was able to remove the contents of the box. Each time he tried, Moroni told him that the time was not yet ready and that he should return in another year. He succeeded on September 22, 1827, and though others tried to steal the gold plates, he took them and fled to his father-in-law's home in Susquehanna, Pennsylvania.

There he began their translation, which he accomplished "from his study of the characters which were magnified before him," with the use of the Urim and Thummin.[32] He "thought [it] out in his mind," and when he "had the assurance that the thought was right, spoke the thoughts in his own words and language to the scribe, from whom he was separated during the process of translation by a curtain."

Mormon doctrines are steeped in faith in visions, prophecies, miracles of healing, and devotion. They call for the active participation, from an early age, of all members of the faith. Mormons are not only concerned with spreading their own gospel, but they are active in establishing its origin in a historical and geographical context.

Since their gospel rests on the prehistory of America as revealed to Joseph Smith, Mormons have made great efforts to establish the geographic background of the *Book of Mormon*. They have sponsored scientifically conducted investigations to gather archaeological information which has been used, along with other sources, for reconstruction.

In addition to the origin of the higher civilizations, another question of uttermost interest to them is the basis of the widespread myth of the bearded white man, known as Quetzalcoatl to the Aztec in Mexico, Kukulcan to the Maya in Yucatan and Guatemala, and Viracocha to the Inca.[33]

Is the myth of his returning to rule to be interpreted as the Mormons have — as the spread of Christianity throughout the world; or as Montezuma accepted Cortés as the representative of Spanish rule over Mexico; and as Atahualpa, the Inca ruler, accepted Pizarro and his 180 followers as gods — until they started acting as men by raping five hundred sacrosanct Virgins of the Sun?[34]

Regardless of what I might think of the origin of the *Book of Mormon* and of Mormon doctrine and beliefs, my contacts with these people in the Southwest led me to admire their accomplishments. Their industry and success in developing the country wherever they settled demonstrated their religious zeal. These traits led to their persecution, first in New York state, then in Ohio and Missouri, and finally in Illinois in 1839. Then in 1845, their leader, Prophet Joseph Smith, was murdered, and the Mormons were forced to seek a new home. They began their epic trek in the midst of winter in 1846, traveled by wagon, horseback, and foot across the country, and arrived two years and five months later in Utah. Foreign immigrants, seeking to join these settlers later, endured even greater hardships by pushing two-wheeled carts and when these broke down, carrying their possessions on their backs, in order to join those who had already begun building in the new land.

The *Book of Mormon* may be accepted on faith alone as the Mormons recommend. Its origin has been explained as a translation by Joseph Smith of gold plates inscribed in "reformed Egyptian — ancient Phoenician" characters.[35] Those represented by Berrett in his history of the church[36] have little resemblance to any known system of signs. They have been described as free-hand transcriptions in the handwriting of Joseph Smith and cannot now be read. Do they represent some of the characters that appeared on the gold plates? Or are they some sort of shorthand used by Joseph Smith to record his thoughts for dictation? Only he could have given the answers.

Skeptics question whether the origin of the *Book of Mormon* was a revelation or an unconscious reconstruction of many facts and ideas, such as takes place in the creation of legends. Had Joseph Smith read (he is reported to have been almost illiterate) or heard someone tell of the archaeological discoveries made before his time? A number of works were available that could have touched off his imagination.

In 1831, the first of the nine monumental folio volumes of the *Antiquities of Mexico* by Lord (Edward King) Kingsborough was published in London.[37] These, appearing during the following seventeen years, not only gave a picture of the Mexican civilizations, largely through their own texts of picture-writing — the Codices — but kept alive the question of the origin of this civilization. The British Israelite Society, in which

Lord Kingsborough, then Edward King, took a leading part, advocated the theory that the highest civilizations in America had been developed by Israelite migrations to the New World. The Spaniards were the first to make these claims as shown by their accounts published a hundred years earlier.

The first account of the Spanish conquest of Mexico in English was that of Francisco López de Gómara (Cortés' secretary), which became available in 1578.[38] Earlier accounts in Spanish provided Europeans with a knowledge of America. That published in Spain in 1552 by Bernal Díaz del Castillo, *The Discovery And Conquest of Mexico*,[39] which covered his experiences from 1517 to 1521, is especially good. It was translated into English in 1800, five years before the birth of Joseph Smith.

An English edition of Clavijero's *Ancient History of Mexico* was published in London in 1787, and an American edition, printed in Richmond, Virginia, appeared in 1806.[40]

The earliest knowledge of the myths of the bearded white man came to the Spanish after 1519, after the conquest of Mexico. While the Codices told much about the customs and the kind of civilization found in parts of America by the Spanish, this information was not generally made known in the English language until after 1830. At that time, Joseph Smith was only twenty-five years old, and from all accounts he had had little formal education. He was, however, an ardent reader of the Bible. He is reported to have made several prophecies, including that of the Civil War, and he was also a hunter of buried treasure.

Did James Churchward come to believe in the creation of Mu, the history of which he recorded by use of a universal language only he could read? Or did he merely create a fictitious method of interpreting symbols which are found in several widely separated areas throughout the world, as further evidence of Mu?

Does the "Cognate Geometric Rock-writing" defined by William Coxon prove that a written language was understood over the entire world as shown by maps composed of pictographs giving the location of prehistoric ruins in Arizona? Or has Coxon only pointed out, with excellent illustrations, worldwide similarities in some signs and designs?

To sum up: Joseph Smith had his Urim and Thummim to aid in his translation of what he called "reformed Egyptian - ancient Phoenician" characters; Churchward and Coxon had "keys" to a universal language which they found had been used in pictographs in the Southwest. Without the aid of something similar — or a Rosetta stone — the difficulty of knowing the meaning of some peculiar things that have shown up in the Arizona State Museum is demonstrated by the Elephant Slabs and the Lead Crosses.

Elephant Slabs

MY INTEREST in the Elephant Slabs began when one of our museum visitors left a pencil sketch of a number of peculiar signs she had copied from some rocks in Oklahoma, along with a book showing several old alphabets. Some of the signs used in the old alphabets and on the Oklahoma rocks were strikingly similar and reminded me of others that had puzzled everyone who had seen them.

The Arizona State Museum has two small stone slabs showing some peculiar signs, including many used as guides to lost treasure, along with drawings of elephants, birds, and a mountain lion. The Elephant Slabs, as they have become known, had come to the museum in 1950 as part of the Gila Pueblo collections. According to the museum records, from data furnished by the late Earl Morris, archaeologist, the "two slabs were found in a ruin on the south side of the Animas River opposite the little settlement of Flora Vista, New Mexico. The late A. M. Amsden purchased both slabs from a boy who lived at Flora Vista." This had occurred, according to Morris, prior to 1910.

Amsden took Morris to the ruin at which the slabs had been found. Morris dated the ruin at A.D. 1100 and later, based on the potsherds (pieces of broken pottery) on the surface of the site. Of the slabs, Morris wrote: "I can see no reason to doubt the authenticity of these specimens, but how to explain them I would not say. In all my experience I have seen nothing similar."

After the slabs had been acquired by the Arizona State Museum, Harold S. Gladwin, former director of Gila Pueblo, wrote on August 11, 1952:

You will have to use your own judgment as to the significance of these two slabs. Most of the archaeologists who saw them ... condemned them immediately as fakes. [Dr. H. P.] Harry Mera [late director of the Laboratory of Anthropology, Santa Fe] thought they might be Mormon tablets which someone had buried with the idea of staging a "revelation."

Mr. Gladwin brought out another possibility about which it is interesting to speculate. He wrote:

In 1929, an old Navajo chief told Mrs. Aileen O'Bryan [Santa Fe folklorist] some of his old legends .... One of them was the tale of what he called the Blue House, in which two Navajo "Calendar Stones" were buried, the ruin being down the San Juan River .... Whether or not the two slabs are the two calendar stones, I do not know, but it is at least suggestive.

These two elephant slabs in the Arizona State Museum collections have peculiar signs incised on them. Both objects are of very hard quartzitic sandstone, approximately one fourth of an inch thick. The signs on both stones are precisely incised (with some sort of a metal tool?), without obvious indications of tool slippage or overcrossing of lines. Specimen A is deeply incised, and the lines appear to have been retraced for the most part. Specimen B is uniformly only faintly incised, and the surface seems "patinated."

Both slabs have the appearance of objects that had come from cave sites (with surfaces darkly stained) rather than from an "open" site (with calcium deposits on the surface). Both specimens have probably been acid-bathed and washed.

ELEPHANT
SLABS

— Arizona State Museum
Cat. No. GP 52–822, 5¾″ x 6″

SLAB A shows an incised mark along the left where it was probably broken from an original, larger stone.

— Arizona State Museum Cat. No. ASM 6–812, 14¼″ x 7¾″

SLAB B represents a stone "hoe" being roughly flaked along the edge of the wider portion, and may be archaeologically dated as not earlier than A. D. 1200–1300(?).

DETAIL OF SLAB A

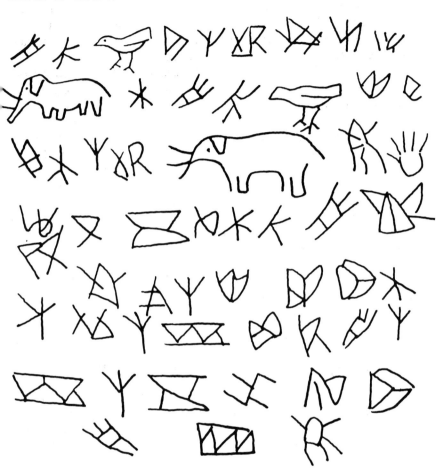

DETAIL OF SLAB B

The connection appeared less likely after Mrs. O'Bryan published a report in 1956,[41] in which she had a diagram of a *single* Calendar Stone based on information revealed by Sandoval, the Navajo chief. This shows the sun, moon, and a list of the twelve months, beginning with October as the first month of the Navajo year and of winter, which lasts through March. April through September compose the summer season.

There is nothing in Mrs. O'Bryan's account of this Calendar Stone nor in the Navajo myths she has reported that suggests that the Elephant Slabs might have any connection with either of them. Mrs. O'Bryan reported that she had been told that the Calendar Stone was hidden in the Carrizo Mountain, which is about seventy-five miles from Flora Vista.

In answer to my inquiry, Mrs. O'Bryan wrote that she had no further information about the Calendar Stone than that contained in her report. But Mr. Gladwin had written earlier that Mrs. O'Bryan's son, Dr. Deric O'Bryan, United States Geological Survey, then surveying archaeological sites within the Mesa Verde National Park, had investigated the possibility of locating the place where the Calendar Stones were hidden. Upon inquiry, Dr. O'Bryan wrote on September 26, 1963:

> Mr. Gladwin was quite right in stating I tried to locate some of the ruins described by old Sandoval to my mother . . . . I felt at the time that I did locate the site the old Navajo called Blue House.
>
> He placed it near the toes of Sleeping Ute Mountain, on the south or east side. There is one quite large and well-preserved Mesa Verde Pueblo in the general area, closer to the Ute's knees than toes and well south of Yucca House at Mesa Verde. Sam Ahkeah, a Navajo, determined that the ruin was called Blue House by the local Indians. It is quite a distance from Flora Vista.

This was all the information I have been able to obtain that even vaguely related to the slabs, although I wrote and asked everyone I could think of for some suggestion as to their origin or meaning. I even asked my Chinese grocery man, who shook his head and replied, "No, not Chinese. No."

The first thing that nearly everyone notices about the slabs is the drawing of the elephants. Elephants were well known in America ten thousand years ago or more. The bones of these animals, along with the stone implements of their hunters, have been found in many places, especially in the Southwest. Some petroglyphs or pictographs of different sorts of strange animals, sometimes identified as mammoths, mastodons, elephants, dinosaurs, lizards, and whatnots have been found. Some appear of recent origin but others may be of pre-Spanish age. There is one example that might represent one or two stylized drawings of what might be an elephant. They are on two fragments of deer bone reported from Jacob's Cavern, near Pineville, Missouri: [42]

Nothing has been discovered and reported in America similar to the pictographs, carvings, and other artifacts made of elephant bones or tusks (and of other extinct animals) that are found in other parts of the world.

But elephants are involved in American folklore. There is a Lago and a Llano de los Gigantes (Lake and Plain of the Giants) in southeastern Chihuahua. The bones of the mammoths found there are enough to prove that giants, maybe monsters, once roamed that part of the country, according to those who have told me about them.

Evidence of the great beast that once lived in a spring just south of the International Border, west of Nogales, was brought to the Arizona State Museum by a Papago Indian; this evidence took the form of a fossil elephant tooth, though the finder described it as a dragon's.

Papago Indian legends tell of the Monster of Quitovac, which once lived in a lake, now dry. It hated people but was finally overcome by the Papago hero, El Primer Montezuma (Iitoi), who was swallowed by the beast. He managed to cut out its heart from within and escape as the monster died.[43]

The origin of the Papago legend may rest in the bones of fossil elephants. But were there any wild elephants living anywhere in America at a later date than ten thousand years ago? Even as late as 1200 A.D., when the ruin at Flora Vista was inhabited?

From the Sierra Madre in western Chihuahua have come tales of a Round Valley, or Green Valley, in which elephants were still living when I heard about them in 1933. One informant would not consider, for any price, showing me the place, as a Mormon had recently been shot and killed there. Another refused because that country was where the followers of Geronimo — the renegade Apache — had hidden out more than fifty years earlier, and he feared that some of these Indians might still be in hiding.

This was the only time I ever heard of wild elephants still living in America. I wondered at the time if, in answer to my questions about elephant bones, my informants were not overly desirous to be helpful.

"¿Quién sabe? Maybe there are elephants somewhere — not here but farther on."

Does the decoration on the pot reportedly found in the Four Corners region where New Mexico, Arizona, Utah, and Colorado now touch represent an elephant without tusks? Is it a part of the original decoration?

THIS PREHISTORIC JAR with an elephant decoration was made about A.D. 1000. It was found about 1885, according to Frederick Bennett Wright.[44] The jar was taken from a ruin in the Montezuma Valley within sight of the spot from which the Elephant Slabs came. According to Wright, nothing else unusual was known to have been found there.

Or was it added, like the floral design to the left of the elephant, which is not a tradition of pottery decoration identified with the Pueblo I Period (about A.D. 1000) in Southwestern archaeology?

Does the pot have any relationship to the Elephant Slabs?

Other representations of what have been considered drawings and sculpture of the heads of elephants have been found in parts of Central and South America. But what had originally been taken for the trunk of an elephant turned out to be the beak of a macaw, the snout of a tapir, or the convolutions of a sea shell. A full account of these and the pros and cons of their identity have been covered in detail by G. Elliot Smith in *Elephants and Ethnologists*.[45]

All sorts of strange beasts representing myths and fantasies have appeared in drawings, sculptures, and pictographs, and have been described in tales in different parts of the world. But no one has ever seemed to have imagined or drawn the likeness of an elephant without having seen or heard about one. As far as I have been able to find out, the drawings on the Elephant Slabs are the only ones in America that have been reported from a prehistoric site.

Besides the drawings of elephants, there are also drawings of birds and a mountain lion (or is it a mouse?), modern Indian signs and symbols, some figures that may be compared with some of the earliest alphabets of about 1100 B.C., treasure hunters' signs, and western cattle brands. A cryptographer, with the help of a philologist, might make some meaning of the signs even though their total number is small.

At my request, White Bear (Oswald Fredericks), the well-known

Hopi Indian painter and writer, made a legendary interpretation of them in May, 1964. With his permission, here are his comments:

The writing is old. During my travels and search for the clan migrations of the Hopi people, the same kind of writing has been found by me, and unknown to others, on the sandstone cliffs of Chaco Canyon, as well as on a large bone.

The writing tells of the Blue Jay Clan, known as the Bird People, who were very close to the Spider Clan at one time. The legends of the Bird People are shown by the writing.

While a few of these people are still living, they have lost most of their old ways. Only one of them, a girl badly wounded, reached Oraibi. The last home of the others was to be west of Moencopi, toward the present town of Page.

The elephants and other animals they saw as they came north out of Central America [are told in the legends of the Bird People who] spoke a different language from that of the Hopi. My Grandmother once sang the songs of the Bird People and my Mother still sings them, but they are so old the meaning is no longer known.

In a different vein, but worthy of consideration, is the interpretation proposed by Don Watson, former Park Service archaeologist. With his permission, here is his letter in answer to my inquiry:

Feb. 2, 1964

Without doubt, I am the only person who can give you an answer. During the years that I was in the archeological business, I found a number of these rock carvings in what is obviously the only written language of prehistoric times north of Mexico. At first I said, as did all the rest of you, "Hoax — fake — Lamanite doodling — piddildy-poop!! But, being able to write unknown languages myself, I decided that perhaps someone else could write unknown languages so I set about deciphering the strange symbols.

It took me a number of years. I found that I could work best in the wee small hours of the morning after copious amounts of coffee had cleared the cobwebs of civilized thinking from my mind and put me back into a slightly more primitive mood. My efforts were crowned with success and at last I was able to read the language with ease. I was preparing a publication on it when I quit the archeological world and went into business. Since then I have been too busy trying to make a living to do anything about it.

In the translations below, I have taken certain liberties. The old language had no verbs, tense or connectives. The symbols, representing things, were just strung together with position being the important portrayer of time and action. I had one bit of trouble with your scripts. My work was with scripts from Mesa Verde while yours were from Aztec which is farther south. Your scripts were written with a decided southern accent which gave me a little trouble. After I realized what the trouble was, I was able to rip through your scripts with ease and here are your translations. And I defy anyone who says I have made the slightest mistake.

A. "I went out to kill a bird this morning with another boy. We had gone a short distance when we had to go around a mammoth in the trail. We killed a bird and started home. We met another mammoth and went around it. Then we realized the two animals were pursuing us. We jumped into a very deep, narrow arroyo and hid. One animal went up the arroyo until he could get down into it, the other went down the arroyo and did the same. We were trapped between them. The charging beasts met head on-with us between them. We were both killed."

B. This is probably the oldest recorded pun and being the first it is, without doubt, the worst. It is pretty awful — you may not even get it.

"When are a bird and a mouse most affectionate? Answer. When they are both inside a lion."

Actually it is a double pun but it would be obvious only to a primitive mind. I guess you won't get it. I didn't!

I am awfully glad to have been able to help you with this — don't hesitate to call on me anytime if you have further problems like this. I certainly believe that one scientist should help another even if it enables you to get all the credit for springing this new ancient language on a startled world.

But seriously, do the signs on the Elephant Slabs have any meaning? To find out, I made a diligent search for any similarities between them and other signs and symbols. I checked the alphabet of Mu, as provided by Churchward. This gave only eleven similarities in *elements* alone, such as the use of lines, angles, squares, rectangles, triangles — no actual similarities between complete signs.[46] The characters, reproduced by Berrett, as appearing on the gold plates from which the *Book of Mormon* was transcribed, show even fewer similarities.[47] Whoever inscribed the Elephant Slabs was not using the universal language of Mu, nor that in which the golden plates of the *Book of Mormon* were written.

But there is a reference to a publication, which I have not seen, but which might be of great use in interpreting the slabs. This was published in 1827 by a John Ranking and is entitled *Historical Researches on the Conquest of Peru, Mexico, Bogotá, Natchez and Talomeco in the 13th Century by Mongols Accompanied With Elephants.*[48] The slabs might even be an account of this conquest carried to the Southwest!

Is there some sort of message on the slabs? The arrangements of the signs in horizontal lines and their frequencies suggest they were not mere doodling. Of the sixty-three signs on the two slabs, there are only three different sequences, two of them in reverse:

The sign ⅄ occurs singly, or combined with other signs, seven times.

The ✗ sign occurs nine times, always combined with some other sign or element:

There are five signs like this,  one reversed; three each of elephants and birds.

Two each of these four signs:

Three variations of the "lotus" (?) design, each repeated once:

The sign ▷ is repeated once in reverse. There are these variations of similar signs:

All other signs occur singly.

It has been suggested to me that the Elephant Slabs are the clue to some hidden treasure that may be interpreted by those who know the meaning of the signs used. Nearly all of the signs can be identified with those used by treasure hunters.[49] The others might be pictographs or Indian designs,[50] some of which are of universal use.[51]

Some of the signs on the Elephant Slabs are similar to those used in some of the earliest alphabets as shown by the following:[52]

—Reproduced with permission of the author, David Diringer, from Figure 52, page 176, *WRITING*, Frederick A. Praeger, Publisher, New York, 1962

NORTH SEMITIC				GREEK				ETRUSCAN		LATIN			MODERN CAPS		
EARLY	EARLY HEBREW	MOABITE	PHOEN.	EARLY	EAST.	WEST.	CLASS.	EARLY	CLASS.	EARLY	MONUM.	CLASS.	BLACK LETTER	ITALIC	ROMAN

DEVELOPMENT of the Alphabet from the North-Semitic of c. 1000 B.C. to modern capitals.

At least a third of the signs on the slabs are similar to registered cattle brands in Arizona and New Mexico: [53]

Post-on-X (or reverse) ✳   X-Bar-R ✗R

Bar-X ✗   X-Y-Slash ✗Y

X-X-Bar ✗-✗   A-Big-A ₳

Bar-X-Bar ✗   Tumbling-R ⱪ

X-Slash ✗✗   Tumbling-Fs ✗✗

Connected-Tumbling-P-Bar-X ⱪ✗

Did some cowboy with a knowledge of ancient alphabets, Indian designs, and treasure hunters' signs incise the slabs?

Similarities in some signs with other categories might also be found. But could any one of these offer a better interpretation than those made by Don Watson or White Bear?

Were the Elephant Slabs only a hoax? If so, a hoax played by whom? And who was the intended victim? Who could have made them and buried them in a ruin at Flora Vista, New Mexico, close to the Aztec National Monument? And what was their purpose?

The earliest white men in the Southwest were the Spaniards. They had little interest, at first, in anything but conquest for loot and for lands to add to the Spanish realm. The first to pass that way must have been Friar Silvestre Velez Escalante and a party of explorers on their way from Santa Fe to Monterey, California, in 1776, searching for a route to connect Spain's northern missions in the New World.[54]

They were followed by American trappers and mountainmen in the early 1800's. They went all over the Southwest, but had their hands full with the job of keeping alive. Little was known of the country until the 1850's, following the California gold rush. Then exploring parties, guided by frontiersmen and sometimes accompanied by soldiers, searched for routes for the pony express and the stagecoach, and later the railroads.

The Mormons had completed their trek to the Great Salt Lake of Utah in the summer of 1848. More were to follow before the outbreak of the Civil War, and shortly afterward, they spread as far south as the Gila River.

Most of the early explorations were to the north or south of the heart of the Indian country — the Four Corners region. After the Civil War, settlers and the United States government began to explore the entire western country — the territorial lands beyond the established states. Among the first of these in the Four Corners region was the Hayden Survey of 1874, sponsored by the Department of Interior.[55]

Like other government expeditions that were to follow, it was made up of scientists, some of whom were interested in archaeology as well as in the living Indians. One of these was the young geologist-artist, William H. Holmes, who afterwards became head of the American Bureau of Ethnology (Smithsonian Institution) and took a prominent part in several fields of anthropology. His report on the *Ancient Ruins of Southwest Colorado, 1875-1876*[56] resulted from his seeing the cliff dwellings in Mancos Valley and was one of the earliest scientific descriptions of them. His greatest interest, however, was in the age of ancient man in America, and during his lifetime he took some part in the discovery or discussion of everything pertaining to the subject.

From the time of this survey, the Four Corners region became the center of attraction for anthropologists in America and elsewhere. Interest was kept alive mainly by the discoveries made by Richard Wetherill, his four younger brothers and his brother-in-law, Charlie Mason, of the many cliff houses in Mesa Verde and the earlier Basketmaker Caves throughout the area.[57]

In 1880 the Wetherill family — Benjamin Kite Wetherill, his wife (Marian Tompkins), and their six children — settled in Southwest Colorado in the Mancos Valley, only forty miles from the Flora Vista ruin. The Colorado gold fever had drawn the family from Kansas, but the five boys and their brother-in-law, led by the oldest brother, Richard, soon were diverted from gold to an even more irresistible lure — the desire to explore the nearby cliff houses. This grew more intense when they discovered the cliff houses within Mesa Verde and when they found the cave sites of the earlier Basketmaker culture. The collections made by the Wetherills were all to find their way into museums. Word of the ruins themselves — spoken and written — attracted every anthropologist in the country, as visitor or investigator.

In 1881, Durango, Colorado, was the end of the Denver and Rio Grande Railroad and the beginning of the trail that led to all other parts of the Southwest. By way of Mancos Valley and the Alamos Ranch of the Wetherills, it went direct to the cliff houses of Mesa Verde and then to the canyons of the San Juan, where the Basketmaker Caves were located.

To the south were the Pueblo Indian villages and the Navajo hogans. The only road was by way of the Animas Valley, past the great Aztec ruins and nearby Flora Vista. Every visitor to the Southwest who came by way of Durango may have passed near the site where the slabs were found prior to 1910.

During the summer of 1891, Baron Gustaf Erik Adolf Nordenskjöld of Sweden visited the Wetherill Ranch in Mancos Valley after seeing a Wetherill collection of pottery, then owned by the Denver Historical Society. After seeing the cliff-dwellings in Mesa Verde, he spent several months with Richard, Al, and John Wetherill excavating a large number of the ruins. Some six hundred specimens were collected and sent to Europe.[58]

This work inspired the Baron to publish *The Cliff Dwellers of the Mesa Verde* at Stockholm in 1893,[59] the first major archaeological work in the United States. It also provided Richard Wetherill and those who worked with him with training in archaeological methods that they used in the years that followed.

Aside from the archaeological work done by the Wetherills and Baron Nordenskjöld the earliest known record of any investigations in the Four Corners area was in 1892. At that time, preparations were being made for the Chicago World's Fair, which opened the next year. Dr. F. W. Putnam, of Harvard University and the Peabody Museum, headed the Anthropological Division of the fair. The exhibit he assembled turned out to be one of the main attractions.[60] Dr. Putnam was one of the most ardent supporters of the theory that man and elephants had been contemporary in America, just as in Europe.

The collecting party for the fair exhibit might well have gone by way of the Animas Valley, which led to the Aztec ruin and nearby Flora Vista, where the Elephant Slabs were found. Could the slabs have been a hoax intended to be uncovered by some member of the field party?

At that time — the 1890's and earlier — American scientists, like those elsewhere, had become involved in the theory of evolution proposed by Darwin and the idea of geological ages demonstrated by Lyell. It was a time of controversies. Opposing sides were drawn, dogmatic in claims and bitter in denunciations.

In Europe, discoveries of stone implements and animal bones were making it apparent that on that continent, man and certain extinct animals, particularly the mammoth, had coexisted. Man's presence in Europe, therefore, went back to very early times. Some archaeologists eagerly sought the same kind of evidence to establish man's antiquity in America. Similarities in stone implements were claimed by some as proof that America, too, could boast of inhabitants as old as any in Europe. Other claims were based on the evidence of artifacts found in alluvium deposits such as those that became known as the "Trenton gravels."[61] Among the archaeologists taking a prominent part in these controversies about the great antiquity of man in America, were both Holmes and Putnam.

Acceptable proof of man's antiquity in America was not found until 1926 with the discovery of "Folsom points" with the bones of extinct bison. In 1932, the older "Clovis points" were found with the remains of mammoth, and later with other extinct species. Since then, numerous other discoveries have been made of the artifacts of ancient man from which archaeologists have established a history of man in America that reaches back for at least twelve thousand years. Some discoveries indicate that man may have been in America as long as twenty-five thousand years ago, or even more, according to some archaeologists.[62]

Before these discoveries, the eagerness of certain archaeologists and the general curiosity of the public created certain demands that were met by fakes. Among these were the Cardiff giant, a twelve-foot figure of a "petrified man" unearthed at Cardiff, New York, on October 16, 1889. Though carved from a block of gypsum, it was first identified as a Phoenician idol, then as the body of an Indian prophet, and was finally declared a fine piece of art.[63] The fakes added more fuel to the scientific controversies.

At the same time that archaeologists were involved in disputes over the age of man in America, ethnologists were just as eager to learn about the aboriginal inhabitants. Theories accounting for the origin of the Indians as migrants from the "lost continents" or as "lost tribes of Israel" from the Old World, had been questioned by most scientists. Some had begun to look to the Indians themselves to find the answers and were especially concerned with the legends, myths, and symbols found among Indian tribes.

Several pioneer investigators with the Smithsonian Institution worked in the area where the Elephant Slabs were found. Dr. Jesse Walker Fewkes was particularly interested in the migrations of the Hopi Indian clans and in the designs on the pottery of the earlier inhabitants of the Hopi country as providing a record of their history. He wrote: [64]

> The pottery from Sikyatki (a large ruin north of the Hopi town of Walpi) is especially rich in picture writing, and imperfect as these designs are as a means of transmitting a knowledge of manners, customs, and religious conceptions, they can be interpreted with good results .... The decipherment of these symbols is in part made possible by the aid of a knowledge of modern survivals, and when interpreted rightly, they open a view of ancient Tusayan (the Hopi) myths, and in some cases of prehistoric practices.

Frank H. Cushing,[65] a pioneer ethnologist also with the Smithsonian, was greatly concerned with Pueblo Indian folk tales. He and other early investigators like Washington Mathews spent months in the Southwest gathering their materials, frequently from Indian informants living in the Four Corners area.

Since these early expeditions and investigations, others have continued exploring and digging in the Southwest. At some time during their stay in the country, some of their members would likely have visited many sites, such as that at Flora Vista.

The late Sherman S. Howe[66] has written an intimate account of his boyhood discovery of the nearby Aztec ruins. His interest in them and early recognition of their significance provide a first-hand account by an untrained but competent observer. But there is nothing in his story that throws any light on the Elephant Slabs.

Like Howe, other early settlers in the Southwest recognized a large part of its archaeology. They frequently called their discoveries to the attention of professionals, as did the Wetherills.

While the ethnologists were interpreting myths and symbols and the archaeologists were wrangling over ancient man in America, some people were still seeking an answer to the question first raised by the Spanish discoverers: were Israelite immigrants to the New World responsible for the high civilization in Meso-America?

The *Book of Mormon* embraced the theory that they were, and the idea was nourished by discoveries and descriptions by John L. Stephens[67] of the spectacular ruins in Mexico and Guatemala. The theory was also believed by Lord Kingsborough.

The Mormons carried the idea with them when they migrated to the Southwest in 1848. They have kept it alive and well-nourished by the research they have sponsored in Meso-America, and especially by the publication of the interpretations they have made of their findings.[68]

The Mormons have frequently been named as responsible for the Elephant Slabs. They were among the first white settlers in that part of the country where they were found. Other stones and pictographs marked with peculiar signs have shown up from time to time in the Southwest, and have also been attributed to this group. Some of the Mormons must have had knowledge of early alphabets, and certainly of pictographs, Indian designs, and cattle brands; treasure hunting was a pastime not unknown to them, either.

Were the slabs made by some Mormon? For what purpose? A hoax?

Other early settlers had the same opportunity, and the slabs might have been planted with the intention of being found by a Mormon. This seems to be the explanation of the Phoenician-like inscriptions on rocks near Las Lunas, New Mexico. The Mormons investigated these writings and concluded that they had been faked by someone as a promotional scheme to raise money to look for Spanish gold.[69]

Or could the slabs have been made and planted as a hoax by someone who knew of the controversy over man's antiquity in America, in hopes that Holmes or Putnam or some other scientist might uncover them? Or were they a hoax, providing a record of myths, clan origins, or migrations of the Pueblo Indians, intended for Cushing or Fewkes or some of their colleagues?

Even scientists are human on occasion and have been known to play practical jokes on one another. It would not be surprising if the idea for the Elephant Slabs originated in some scientific mind, and if they were intended to convey a message it may yet be deduced.

Or are they only recent doodles showing elephants, birds, mountain lions, spiders, and tracks of bears and snowshoes, with some signs that resemble ancient alphabets, Indian designs, treasure hunters' symbols, and cattle brands?

Or do they truly record some prehistoric American's account of elephants? Or of legends of the people who once lived in the Southwest? Or of something buried at the Flora Vista ruin?

The answer is yet to be found.

After more than forty years as an archaeologist, I've seen quite a few peculiar things. Most of them can be explained, but the Elephant Slabs remain a puzzle. How much more of a puzzle might have been made of them is shown by the story of the Lead Crosses.

Lead Crosses

SOME PECULIAR METAL OBJECTS, shaped like crosses, swords, spears, and batons found near Tucson, are now a part of Southwestern legends. Their discovery in 1924 created a newspaper controversy that lingers on.

The Lead Crosses, as the strange objects became known, were decorated with Christian crosses, Moslem crescents, Hebraic seven-branched candle sticks, Freemasonry symbols, and other signs. There were also Latin phrases, as well as Hebrew.

"A few are broken, as though done in combat," one news story reported, "and the general disposition of these finds portrays the confusion of a pitched battle."

A translation of the inscriptions on the Lead Crosses was interpreted as a record left by a band of Roman-Jews who came to America, which they called *Calalus,* in the latter part of the eighth century. The interpretations gave a history of conflict between the kingdom they had established in the Southwest and the Toltec Indians of Mexico from 775 A.D. to 900 A.D.

Another interpretation identified the crosses with Coronado and other Spanish explorers of the Southwest. The Spanish were said to have obtained the objects from the Crusaders, who had brought them to Spain from the Holy Land.

Simultaneous feature story coverage of the discovery of the Lead Crosses on December 13, 1925, started a bitter war of words between the *Arizona Daily Star* and the *New York Times* and other papers, as well as between individuals in different parts of the country. The story of the discovery filled three pages of the *Star's* Sunday edition. Its front page gave the story a banner headline. Lead articles were signed by Clifton J. Sarle, Ph.D., Mrs. Laura Coleman Ostrander, and a *Star* staff writer, Gilbert Cosulich, all of Tucson.

A log of the excavations showed that the objects had been unearthed by Charles E. Manier in September, 1924, on the property of Thomas W. Bent, both of Tucson, at a lime kiln on the Silver Bell Road, about seven miles from the heart of the city.

The feature contained full reproductions of the artifacts and translations of their inscriptions. The *Star* gave full support to the interpretation by Mrs. Ostrander, a history teacher, who said that the crosses were a record of Roman-Jewish settlement in America in the eighth century.

That they had been unearthed as described by the original discoverers was verified by Frank Fowler, professor of classical literature, A. E. Douglass, Director of the Steward Observatory, Dean Byron Cummings, Director of the Arizona State Museum, and Charles T. Vorhies, all of the University of Arizona. All had been present at the removal of one of the crosses from the earth, and Dean Cummings verified that the objects came from the gravel deposit at the lime kiln. The literal translations of the Latin inscriptions on all the objects were published by the *Star* in its announcement of the discovery. The following is a free translation of the text on the cross shown:

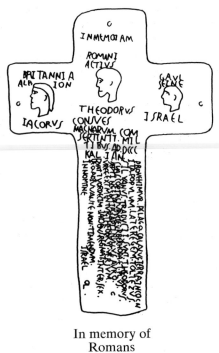

	In memory of	
Britain	Romans	Gaul
Albion	Actius	Seine
Jacob	Theodore	Israel

Consuls of Great Cities With 700 soldiers on January 1, 800 A.D.
Vertical: Go over the sea to Calalus, an unknown land, where a people (the Toltecs) are ruled by Silvanus.

Theodore brings up his forces at the City of Rhoda and captures 700. No gold is taken from the city. Theodore, a man of great courage, rules 14 years, Jacob rules 6 years.

With God's help nothing need be feared in the name of Israel. O L (historian's initials)

ROMAN RELICS FOUND HERE BAFFLE SCIENCE

LEAD CROSSES, SCARRED SWORDS 1200 YEARS OLD, ARE GENUINE, DECLARE LOCAL ARCHAEOLOGISTS

Leaden Relics May Mean New Chapter of History

Roman Jews in 'Terra Calalus,' America, from 775 A. D. to 900 An Announcement of the Discovery of Leaden Artifacts Bearing Inscriptions in Latin and Hebrew, Now Being Unearthed Near Tucson, Arizona.

By Clifton J. Sarle, Ph.D., and Mrs. Laura Coleman Ostrander.

Leaden artifacts of great antiquity have been unearthed near Tucson, Arizona, during the past year. All of the objects bear significant drawings; a number of them inscriptions in Latin and two in both Hebrew and Latin. Many dates also are given. The story revealed opens a new chapter in the pre-Columbian history of America. It is a record of a colonization in America by Europeans. In 775 A.D., and a brief chronicle of their life here, covering a period of 125 years.

To many, on first consideration, the claim that the Atlantic was crossed and American colonized by Mediterranean people, 717 years before the coming of Columbus, will seem preposterous. But to others, however startling this discovery may seem, it will appear quite in line with the volume of evidence gleaned in recent years in various fields of investigation, which points convincingly to Old and New World maritime intercommunication back even into the centuries B.C.

Cross Found Near Tucson

A chance find by Mr. Charles E. Manier of a pair of large leaden crosses protruding from a gravel stratum near the base of a low-lying bluff which flanks the westerly side of the flood-plain of the Santa Cruz river for several miles below Tucson, was the beginning of this most important discovery. The Silver Bell highway follows approximately the boundary line between this bluff and the flood-plain, and one traveling this road passes a number of old lime kilns, long abandoned, which were built into the face of this bluff. On September 13, 1924, Mr. Manier, accompanied by his father, who was visiting him from California, was returning along this road from an auto ride, when at the station of the latter, they stopped to examine one of these old lime kilns, like the one structed by die like pit in the which the bluff tr...

To Exhibit Relics For Chest Fund This Afternoon

The relics that have been discovered on the Silverbell road by Thomas W. Bent and Charles E. Manier will be placed on exhibition this afternoon at the headquarters of the Tucson Community Chest, in the Tucson bank building, Bent and Mainer announced last night.

The placing of the exhibit has been authorized by Mayor John E. White, chairman of the chest campaign.

An admission charge of 25 cents for adults and 10 cents for children will be made. Half of the proceeds will go to the Community Chest and the other half will be used for further excavations and research, in the effort to clear up the mystery of the "Calalus" finds.

INSCRIBED WITH LATIN, HEBREW

Accidentally Unearthed by C. E. Manier and T. W. Bent

MAY CHANGE HISTORY

Left by Race 700 Years Before Columbus Landed, Belief

By GILBERT COSULICH

Graven in Latin and in Hebrew upon ancient crosses and battered swords, a new chapter of early American history, which some scholars declare will prove that Europeans lived and fought and died in Arizona 700 years before Columbus landed at San Salvador, has just been unearthed near Tucson.

The objects that have been excavated bear dates ranging from 560 A. D. to 900 A. D. These relics—left in zona, according to by a band of F ers who

warn of many seasons had expose the ends of these cross side of the cut and Manier's

The *New York Times,* on the same date as the *Star,* announced the discovery of the crosses in a two-page spread. The *Times* gave a full account of the discovery and a description, but cast doubt on the authenticity of the finds and bolstered its stand by quoting certain eastern scientists. Bashford Dean, Curator of Arms and Armor at the Metropolitan Museum of Art, who had made a lifelong study of forgeries, looked at photographs of the Lead Crosses and announced that they would rank among the poorest of forgeries.

F. W. Hodge, a specialist in archaeology and the history of the Southwest from the Museum of the American Indian, Heye Foundation, thought it was probable that an archaeological faker who had been making false inscriptions of Coronado and Fray Marcos de Niza in Arizona had something to do with the Tucson find.

Neil Merton Judd, anthropologist and curator of American Archaeology of the United States National Museum, made an investigation of the site and the Lead Crosses. Although he professed full confidence in Dean Cummings' ability and judgment, he felt that the crosses were not as old as the dates on them would indicate and were probably no older than 1540.

The lines had been drawn and the journalistic struggle had started. The *Star* supported the claim that the crosses were genuine, though their origin might be unknown. The *Times* took the opposite stand.

The next day, December 14, the *Times* quoted C. H. Marvin, President of the University of Arizona, as saying, "We are going to work on the problem to prove or disprove it."

Still more doubting scientists, from the American Museum of Natural History and Columbia University, were quoted at length.

The widespread interest in the discovery was shown in an Associated Press release from New York, also on the 14th, quoting James T. Shotwell, professor of history at Columbia, who pointed out that while the relics contained dates such as A.D. 775, the Anno Domini system did not come into general use until about A.D. 1000. The *Times* smugly reported the next day that a Joseph Wheless, in a note to the paper on the 14th, had pointed out the paradox and it had been confirmed by Dr. Shotwell.

The *Star,* undaunted, countered the *Times'* skepticism with the announcement on the 15th, that the University would have charge of the completion of the excavation, the work to start after the holidays, with Dean Cummings in charge.

On the same date, the *Star* rustled up some support for its position by referring to an article in the July, 1925, issue of *Improvement Era,* the official publication of the Mormon Church. The author, J. M. Sjodahl, former editor of the *Deseret News,* Salt Lake City, Utah, was quoted as saying that he considered the inscriptions on the crosses "exceedingly significant and have a significant bearing upon the Mormon claim that descendants of the Lamanites crossed to the American continent."

Although the *Star* recognized the *Times* stunning coup, with its evidence of the dating error, the *Star* promptly quoted Dr. O. A. Turney, a

Phoenix archaeologist, who believed the Lead Crosses were "bonafide, but not pre-Spanish."

By now the *Tucson Daily Citizen* had leaped into the fray, taking sides with the *Times* against its rival. The *Citizen's* headline revealed that "RELIC TEXTS ARE CRIBBED FROM DICTIONARY GLOSSARY." In a long article signed by E. S. Blair of Tucson, a Cornell Law School graduate, student of Latin, and former practicing attorney in New York City, the *Citizen* pointed out that several of the inscriptions contained modern English and French words such as "Gaul" and "Seine"; that the Latin was classical, not eighth century; and that Hebrew was not "known or studied by Christians in Europe" in the eighth century. Furthermore, the style of the lettering of the inscriptions indicated that they were probably copied from recorded history.

Regardless of these setbacks, the *Star* proudly pointed out in an editorial that it was the first to announce the discovery of the relics that were now causing so much interest — and heated discussion — in the archaeological world as well as among laymen. The first account, dated September 21, 1924, was headlined "TABLETS FOUND HERE BEAR INSCRIPTION OF 800 A.D." In spite of tremendous opposition, the *Star* had not weakened.

Meanwhile, back at the university, Dean Cummings had packed up some of the crosses and headed east to show them to other scientists.

On December 17, 1925, the *Star* hopefully sounded a Phoenician theme by giving the opinion of a former attorney general of Ohio. "Phoenician sailors, the navigators of the Semitic people, is the logical answer to the cache of artifacts . . ., according to Wade H. Ellis, member of the National Archaeological Society at Washington, who was in the city last night."

But on the 20th, the *Times* summed up its side of the argument with a full-page story recounting some of the proven fakes of the past. Of these, the Cardiff giant, mentioned earlier, was perhaps the most celebrated hoax in the country.

The *Star* began to show some signs of weakening in an editorial on December 21, summarizing the nationwide skepticism of others. "Against this flood of doubt," it stated that it had found support only by "some local scientists," chief of whom was Dean Cummings, "who was still determined to get the facts."

Two days later, though, the *Star* became defiant with an article by Gilbert Cosulich.

IF DEAN CUMMINGS SAYS THEY'RE GENUINE, THEY ARE, DECLARE TUCSONANS. Harold Bell Wright, Albert Steinfeld, Mayor John E. White and Mrs. Allie Dickerman among Those Who Back Relics.

"Articles probably buried by some one shortly after the coming of Cortés to the New World," Steinfeld said. Carl R. Tisor, Assistant U.S. Attorney, believed the artifacts are genuine. A. H. Condron, Secretary of Tucson Chamber of Commerce, "concurs."

Mrs. Allie Dickerman, postmistress, is quoted to believe in Dean Cummings and Dr. A. E. Douglass.

Harold Bell Wright: "I don't know anything about the artifacts, but I do believe in Dean Cummings." Miss Fanny Strassman, Harold Bell Wright's secretary: "I don't know anything about the artifacts, but I do believe in Mr. Wright."

Miss Rose Braun, Secretary County Agricultural Extension: "Believe." Leslie D. Rhea, Insurance Salesman: "What is good enough for Dean Cummings, is good enough for me."

Then on December 26, while Dean Cummings was exhibiting the crosses to the eastern skeptics, the *Star* showed a bit of pique with one of the dean's relatives. *"Uncles, Nephews, and Relics,"* the paper entitled an editorial proclaiming that while Dr. Neil M. Judd of the U.S. National Museum, a nephew of Dr. Cummings, still straddled the fence, Tucson would believe the artifacts were genuine until they were proved otherwise.

On January 5, the *Star* recovered more optimism after publishing a telegram that had been received by Mr. Bent from Dean Cummings: "Presented Tucson Finds. Nobody scoffed. Many interested." But the puzzle of the Lead Crosses was further complicated by January 15. With a headline, "SCULPTOR ONCE LIVED ON SITE OF ARTIFACTS," the *Star* reported that Leandro Ruiz, a retired pioneer cattleman, had been acquainted forty years before with a young Mexican sculptor named Odohui, who lived at the lime kiln where the crosses were discovered. Ruiz suggested that the relics might have been some of his work.

Five days later the *New York Times* elaborated the story. The sculptor's father, Vicente, was well educated and cultured, possessing a classical library. The son, Timotéo, molded objects in metal and carved in stone, and was greatly interested in buried treasure.

The family lived at the lime kiln for eight or nine years. After the death of the father, the widow and son disappeared and were thought to have returned to Mexico. Eduardo Machado, also of Tucson, corroborated Ruiz' story.

The *Star* airily dismissed the idea that the crosses were false and welcomed Dean Cummings home with the announcement, on January 19:

CUMMINGS FIRMER THAN EVER IN BELIEF TUCSON ARTIFACTS ARE GENUINE.

Dean Cummings reported that the crosses had been received with gratifying interest, in spite of skepticism in Kansas City where they had been shown at a meeting of the American Association for the Advance-

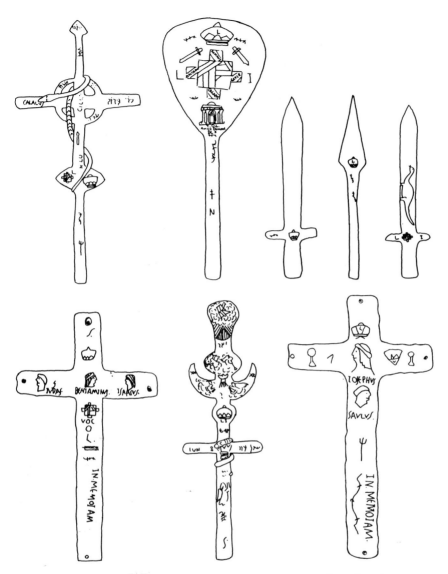

THE LEAD CROSSES were "cast of lead and antimony alloy showing traces of tin, gold, silver and copper," Dean Cummings reported in the *Arizona Daily Star*, January 19, 1926. "Ores of this character were mined in the Tucson mountains and other mountains farther to the south. The ores had probably been crushed and crudely smelted, the metals puddled and then used." ". . . most of the articles have been cast and then shaped by hammering and smoothing . . . the engraving has been done by a sharp point with a straight stroke. All are crudely fashioned and show such work as might be expected to be produced by men in the desert country of Arizona with few tools and no mechanical appliances," the article reported.

ment of Science. There was concerted opposition to them, however, by the Washington Academy of Science. The article pointed out that Dean Cummings "did not seem disturbed by the recent suggestion that the relics might have been made by a young Mexican sculptor."

The information about the sculptor must have raised questions in the minds of some of the *Star's* supporters; it certainly gave more support to the detractors. But on February 18, Mrs. Ostrander, the history teacher who had originated the Roman-Jewish settlement idea, came up with a new theory.

"Quetzalcoátl, 'the bearded white man' whom the Toltec Indians of Mexico worshipped as their god, may have been Israel III, leader of the mysterious wanderers who are believed by some to have left the leaden artifacts recently unearthed near Tucson," she is reported to have pointed out in an address before the American Association for the Advancement of Science in Phoenix.

By now the *Star* was struggling mightily to maintain its earlier mood as declared in its editorial on December 21, 1925: "Whatever the weight of evidence on either side of the mystery, we must frankly admit that we hope the artifacts are genuine."

It must have given up this hope, however, when it reported on March 1, 1926:

Financial support of the University of Arizona for the further excavation and exploration of the land along the Silver Bell Road upon which the artifacts believed to be of pre-Columbian origin, were found by Charles Manier and T. W. Bent, has been withdrawn, according to an announcement last night by Dean Byron Cummings of the University.

The cause of the withdrawal by the University was given as hinging on failure to agree with the owners of the land regarding the disposal of the artifacts which may be unearthed in the future. Cummings declared that it was the proposal of the University to finance the excavation of the land and divide the artifacts which may be unearthed on an equal basis between Manier and Bent and the Arizona State Museum, but upon further negotiations with them they refused to accept the terms of the University, he said.

But interest in the Lead Crosses had not died, for the *Citizen,* in its afternoon edition that day, reported that according to Charles Manier, "An out-of-town financier, with a hobby of scientific research, has become interested in the so-called Hebrew-Latin artifacts, and is expected to finance further excavations at the lime kiln on Silver Bell Road."

The *Star* editorial of March 4 showed that the paper had lost more sympathizers. The editorial reported that the discoverers of the crosses had objected to an earlier *Star* editorial, claiming it gave a false impression that the University had been defraying all expenses of the investigation and that the University had control of the work that had been done. A letter to the editor, signed by Thomas W. Bent, for himself and Charles E. Manier, stated: "This is not so. The investigation to date has been under the supervision of Dr. C. J. Sarle, Mrs. Laura Coleman Ostrander, Mr. C. E. Manier, Mr. J. S. Bent and myself, with a few members of the University faculty acting in an advisory capacity."

With the headline, "THREE LATIN TEXT-BOOKS CONTAIN ALL PHRASES ON ARTIFACTS," the *Star* capitulated on March 7. The story pointed out that, according to Dr. Frank Fowler of the University, all the inscriptions on the relics could be found in *Harkness Latin Grammar,* the *Latin Grammar of Allen and Greenough,* and Rouf's *Standard Dictionary of Facts* (earliest edition of 1864).

The *Star* also reported: "Dean Cummings yesterday expressed a possibility that the tablets may have been buried by a member of the Mormon faith to perpetuate the story given in the Book of Mormon which claims the Indians of America as direct descendants of the ancient Israelites."

The final scores rung up by those taking sides in the controversy that started with the announcement on December 13, 1925, of the discovery of the Lead Crosses, were:

Explanations of their origin offered by the *Arizona Daily Star* and those who sided with it:

They recorded a Roman-Jewish settlement in America from 775 A.D. to 900 A.D.;

They recorded the presence of the Phoenician sailors in America, who had brought the Lost Tribes of Israel here;

They were left by Coronado's followers, either as relics picked up by the Spanish Crusaders or as a hoax;

They substantiated the *Book of Mormon;*

They were "planted" by someone as a hoax to substantiate the *Book of Mormon;*

They were a record of Quetzalcoatl, the bearded white man of Mexican legends.

Against their "authenticity" were the claims of the *New York Times* and those who sided with it:

They were incorrectly dated, in using "A.D." before it had become customary;

The inscriptions contained modern words and were taken from recent text-books;

The relics may have been made by a Mexican sculptor who had lived at the lime kiln, had access to a classical library, and was known to be a treasure hunter;

Other archaeological hoaxes and fakes had been found in the past and these were described in order to further the claims of the doubters.

No one, according to the newspaper accounts, ever questioned the fact that the Lead Crosses came from the gravel-caliche beds at the lime kiln as reported by their discoverers and as witnessed by others. But how did they get there, and why, and who made them? These questions have never been satisfactorily answered.

If anyone quoted by the papers harbored any opinions other than those reported, I do not know of them. This summary is based solely on what the newspapers reported from December 13, 1925, to March 7, 1926.

Many of those who took part in the newspaper controversy are no longer living. As it is reviewed from a later time and by an outsider, it is easy to understand how the newspaper accounts of the Lead Crosses created so much interest forty years ago; it is easy to understand, particularly, that they should have been the subject of so much adverse speculation.

Had I known about them when the controversy raged, my sympathy would have been with the *Star* and those who worked to determine their origin and meaning, rather than with those who set out to condemn them before they could be investigated.

There is no record of how many newspapers carried the story from its first appearance until the controversy subsided or how many times the story has been retold in print in the following years. During the time I was curator of the Arizona State Museum, countless visitors asked about the crosses and wanted to see them. They are not in the Arizona State Museum as has been reported in several publications; from last accounts, they still belong to the discoverers. They should be preserved in some Arizona museum. They are as much a part of the state's heritage as are the myths and legends that have enriched it, as the documents of its historical backgrounds, and the records of its archaeological past.

The *Star,* in an editorial on December 15, 1925, expressed what is likely to have been the opinion of most of those who took part in the controversy: "Wherever the relics are placed in history, their worth cannot be depreciated by hasty decisions."

The story of the Lead Crosses still lives, as the *Star* reminisced in an editorial of December 14, 1963 on "a Tucson hoax." It will continue to live as long as people are interested in peculiar things. The Lead Crosses have become as much a part of the Southwest as is the story of the horned toad found in the cornerstone of the Eastland County Courthouse in Texas, thirty-one years after it was built.

Fakes and Frauds

IF THE LEAD CROSSES originated as a hoax, their discovery stirred up a greater commotion than their creator might have anticipated. That seems to be the way of other hoaxes.

When Coronado was led on a search for Gran Quivira and greater wealth than the Seven Silver Cities possessed, his informant, The Turk, confessed that he had started the Spaniards wandering over the plains of Texas and finally into Kansas so that he might be escorted safely home. But Coronado wasn't amused, and The Turk was strangled.

This ending of what might have started as a hoax hasn't dampened the spirits of Texans four hundred years afterwards, as shown by the story of "Old Rip," a horned toad that was reported to have been removed from the cornerstone of the Eastland County Courthouse, thirty-one years after it had been built. Here is the way it came about, according to Mr. Herbert J. Tanner, of Eastland, Texas:

In 1897, when the cornerstone of the then new courthouse was dedicated, Ernest Wood, Justice of the Peace, a member of the band, noticed his son Will playing with a horned toad. Ernest Wood decided to place the toad in the cornerstone. On February 28, 1928, when the old courthouse was demolished, three thousand persons watched the opening of the cornerstone to see if the horned toad was still alive. Judge Ed. S. Pritchard removed the Bible and other objects, and, at the bottom, was Old Rip. Eugene Day, an oil man, reached into the cavity and lifted up a dust-covered toad, which he handed to the Reverend Frank S. Singleton, who handed it to Judge Pritchard, who held it up by its leg so that all might see. Suddenly the other leg twitched. The toad was alive! The crowd cheered, and thus Old Rip awoke from his thirty-one year slumber.

Mr. Tanner wrote on October 11, 1963: "I am sure that today you could find over a thousand good Eastland Citizens who would bear witness to its authenticity."

Old Rip lived for only a year after his celebrated appearance; he died of pneumonia on Saturday, January 19, 1929. His body was embalmed and placed in a beautiful, plush-lined casket in the lobby of Eastland County's new courthouse. But before he died, the news of Old Rip was spread far and wide.

Dr. Julius Olsen, then of Hardin-Simmons University, Abilene, is reported to have said, "I think it is quite probable the frog could have lived that long under the conditions, although I have never heard of a similar case before."

The Honorable Andrew J. Volstead of St. Paul, Minnesota, former congressman and father of the prohibition enforcement act, is said to have exclaimed: "Thirty-one years without a drink! I think that toad should be heartily commended." Then he showed an element of doubt when he added: "Provided he isn't an imposter."

The Honorable Barry Miller of Austin, acting governor of Texas, said it was hard to believe, but he vouched for the endurance qualities of the ugly little reptile generally.

Dr. D. W. Hamlett of Bloomington, Indiana, assistant professor of zoology at Indiana University, expressed skepticism: "Thirty-one years would seem to be about 29 years too long."

Drs. D. B. Castell and J. T. Patterson of Austin, University of Texas professors, would not comment definitely but leaned toward skepticism.

Dr. Raymond L. Dittmars of New York, curator of the New York Zoological Gardens, and Dr. William H. Mann of Washington, D.C., Director of the National Zoological Park, both said "absolutely impossible."

The Smithsonian Institution in Washington branded Old Rip as a fraud. "Horned toads positively cannot live for more than a few days without sunlight."

Paramount Newsreel Company is reported to have come to Eastland and recorded a re-enactment of the scene for distribution throughout the United States. And Ripley featured Old Rip twice in his "Believe it or Not" series.

In May, 1928, Old Rip was exhibited in various parts of the United States and was brought to entertain President Coolidge, who is reported to have broken several other engagements in order to get a glimpse of the toad. But even Old Rip couldn't get the tight-lipped president to make any comment.

However, Old Rip's memory lives on. An Annual Eastland Old Rip Horned Toad Derby was first held on July 16, 1949. Some of the early winners are reported to have been entries of the Honorable James Farley, former postmaster general, and those of Charlie McCarthy and Mortimer Snerd.

Old Rip was never proven to be a hoax, nor were sides taken as with the Lead Crosses. Probably it was only a hoax, but one that was not intended for any one individual. It was accepted by all in good spirit — just a practical Texas joke.

The Lead Crosses and the Elephant Slabs may have been hoaxes, but no satisfactory explanation has been made of their purpose, nor of their origin.

Just how and why a hoax may be started is shown by the following account of the Goddess of Fertility.

GODDESS OF FERTILITY

IN THE SUMMER OF 1948 — and before and after — the Arizona State Museum and the Department of Anthropology of the University of Arizona conducted an archaeological field school at Point of Pines, on the San Carlos Apache Indian Reservation in eastern Arizona. (The field school, since located at Grasshopper, an ancient ruin on the Fort Apache Indian Reservation, received a nationwide coverage when the daughter of President Lyndon Baines Johnson, Miss Lynda Bird Johnson, spent two weeks in the summer of 1965 as a student at the school project. Among other things, she excavated a burial site and a fire pit).

Among the students present in the summer of 1948 was a young Hungarian with the courtly manners of his aristocratic European background. His arrival in polished black boots, full peg-legged riding breeches, and a Tyrolean cloth hat with a feathered cockade, was received with mixed feelings by the other students whose backgrounds were largely of the Southwest.

To some, each time Steve, as he was soon called, bowed low, it was an invitation for a swift kick. At the same time, there was just as strong a feeling of sympathy and a desire to help with his halting English and his lack of knowledge of American customs. Although his mannerisms were alien to them — as theirs no doubt were to him — they knew that he was honest, sincere, friendly, and capable.

Steve was given a place to work excavating a room in the large ruin with other beginners. What he wanted most to find was a Mexican figurine. He spent weeks in removing the fill of earth and stones from the ground level marked by four rows of rocks — indicating the walls — to a depth of more than six feet. This was the first time he had felt the hard wooden handle of a shovel in his hands, though he had supervised important archaeological digs in Europe as a staff member of the Hungarian National Museum. As the hole he was digging grew deeper, the weather grew hotter and stickier, for the summer rains were due shortly. The rains had started when Steve finally reached what should have been the floor level. There he found the bottom of his excavation covered with large pieces of broken pottery, all lying flat. He carefully brushed off his finds ready to explore what might be below when a shower put four inches of water in his excavation.

The next day Steve began bailing out the muddy water. He sweated in the hot sun, working barefooted in the black, sticky muck. When he griped to the dig foreman, he was pushed the harder to clean up the mess before another shower would make him do his work over again. The only sympathy he received was from the camp cook who spent his off-hours watching the dirty work progress.

Several days passed before Steve was ready to investigate what lay beneath the sherds that covered the floor. He carefully raised one larger than the others, near a corner, to see what was beneath, as he had been told to do in case photographs should be needed to record an important find. He took one look and hastily replaced the sherd. Without a word to others nearby, he hurried back to the laboratory where the director and others, including some distinguished visitors, were at work.

Breathlessly he announced, "Doc, I have something you must see."

"What?" asked the director, as the others all stared at the excited Steve.

"A Mexican figurine — made of ivory — come!"

Curious, all the laboratory workers, the photographer, the dig foreman, and the student diggers on the ruin gathered to watch, as word had passed that Steve had found the Mexican figurine he had talked about all summer. It was something never before found in that part of the Southwest. Steve had made the big discovery!

As the work progressed, the interest increased. Pictures were taken of every step in the uncovering of the spectacular find. Finally the big sherd was removed and the black muck beneath it carefully brushed clean, revealing more of the gleaming ivory-like object that lay in a matrix of black, damp soil. It was an ivory-white figure of a long-legged female. Not until more photographing, more mapping, and more note-taking was the find carefully removed.

It was a figure of a slender girl, scantily dressed, with a greatly extended abdomen, standing on a pedestal bearing the inscription, KILROY WAS HERE! — all made of plastic.

Someone had planted it on Steve.

He felt ridiculed. He was miserable during the following days when anyone brought up the subject of his find, or when anyone even looked at him.

Everyone wondered who would do such a thing to Steve. The director declared that the perpetrator of the joke could confess and would be absolved. But no one seemed to know how the hoax had found its way into Steve's dig — at least no one confessed.

Tensions were building up until finally, at an evening meal, when the hungry students filed in to the dining room, the tables were all bare except for the usual place settings and filled water glasses. The director alone was served a fried chicken dinner, with home-made hot rolls and all the trimmings — with a warning from the cook to save room for ice cream and cake. Only dry crackers were placed on all the other tables.

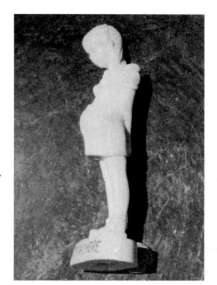

The Goddess of Fertility

THE MOMENT OF DISCOVERY of a great find is watched by students in the University of Arizona Field School of Archaeology.

After the director was half through his meal, he rose and, after looking sternly into the hungry faces of the others, said, "That is all you should have to eat until the guilty one has confessed." He explained how serious it was to tamper with the archaeological record, even with so obvious a hoax as the plastic figurine that Steve had found. He sat down to continue his meal. The others stared at one another and glared at Steve, who blushed pink.

It was not until later when the cook appeared carrying a big tray loaded with fried chicken, followed by the kitchen helpers loaded with other trays, that all relaxed — and ate. Even Steve seemed finally to realize that it was only a practical joke. The old-timers, who had spent their lives in the Southwest, had tried to convince him that he had actually been honored by the other students — or whoever had planted the figurine — in being selected for an initiation to become one of them as eastern "dudes" were once initiated by western cowboys. At that time the method was a rough handling, but if the victim could take it, he was accepted. If not, he usually disappeared without a word — a good riddance, in the way of western thinking.

Steve showed that he could take it, even if he kept on kissing ladies' hands. Before the school session ended, he was just one of the group that lived together and learned to get along and to like one another. From there, Steve went on to work in Guatemala, and then to study and teach in American universities. Today, Steve is well known as Dr. Stephen F. Borhegyi, director of the Milwaukee Public Museum, the fourth largest natural history museum in the country.

This is only one account of hoaxes of one sort or another that have been played on fellow archaeologists. How many others have not been uncovered by the intended victims? This one was obviously a plant — but did the Lead Crosses and the Elephant Slabs originate in a similar way? If so, they apparently were not found by the intended victims, and they continue to baffle everyone who knows about them.

Who planted the hoax on Steve? No one ever confessed. It might have been only one of the group, or it could have been several. Maybe most of the school was in on it. There is one only thing of which I am fairly sure — that Steve did not join in playing the trick on himself. And I am certain that I did not have anything to do with it until I made the photographic record of the uncovering of Steve's great find.

But suppose the hoax had not been so obviously a practical joke or that it had not been discovered? Then it might have become another peculiar thing such as the Lead Crosses and the Elephant Slabs. It might even have been interpreted as a clue to legendary treasure, just as the slabs and the crosses were.

Swindles

A HOAX MAY BE only a practical joke in the mind of the perpetrator, but it can be a cruel experience for the victim. It can smother pretenders with ridicule, as nothing is more upsetting to a "stuffed-shirt" than a deflated ego. Though jokes may sometimes be harsh, they are also a rough and direct way to reveal character — of both victim and perpetrator.

A hoax succeeds when it fulfills some desire of the victim, whether it is to confirm an idea or to promise some material gain. The easiest dupe for the con man is the greedy, not-too-conscientious person, who thinks he can always get something for nothing.

Buried treasures and lost mines have become the bait for some swindles. The most common are the sale of treasure maps — not those showing general locations according to legends, but those which are represented as giving the secret location of a specific treasure along with its history — all for a whopping price. Since hunters of buried treasures and lost mines have been known to guard their secrets with their lives, any offer for the sale of information should be suspect.

Sometimes the sucker is urged to put up cash for a liberal share in a treasure, such as the ever-popular "Treasure of the Mexican Prisoner." In this swindle, the confidence operators work this way: the contact man sells the idea to some gullible victim, promising to share a fortune with him, *if* the victim will advance a few thousand dollars to free a prisoner from a Mexican jail, who alone knows the hiding place of a fabulous treasure. His freedom is the price he asks to share in the fortune.

The prisoner may really exist — a confederate actually in a Mexican jail. Proof of the treasure is in the samples of rich ore, bullion, or coins, supplied by the contact man and shown to the victim. Of course, the conspirators insist, the transaction must be kept secret since Mexican officials need to be bribed to free the prisoner and, again, to aid in smuggling the treasure across the border into the United States. Time will be needed to do all these things *after* the money has been paid — time for the confidence men to disappear! And that's the end of the story — until the same fraud is played on somebody else in much the same fashion!

More common than swindles of this type are the multitude of faked artifacts — frequently represented as authentic primitive art — which occasionally come to rest in some museum. More often they are brought to a museum by their owners, seeking verification of their rarity and

119

authenticity, and hoping that their value is at least as much as the price paid. Some collectors are governed primarily by the desire to own something unique, and there always seems to be someone around to supply their needs.

To the archaeologist who is asked to pass on the prized object, it is immediately suspect. No matter how genuine it may appear, it may be a fraud unless something closely resembling it has been unearthed by an experienced archaeologist. But some fraudulent wares may be better art than the originals.

On my trips to Mexico, I have always been offered the chance to buy "antiques" while visiting the ruins. Some of the things offered for sale by the swarm of peddlers are genuine — fragments of clay figurines and pieces of broken pottery commonly found on trash mounds. Whole pieces are usually poor fabrications so obvious that I wonder why anyone buys them, much less cherishes them as primitive art.

But on one of my visits to Teotihuacán, the great group of ruins outside of Mexico City, I acquired my sole piece of primitive art.

It was early in the day, before the crowds of tourists had arrived, when a ragged little boy of ten, under a straw hat much too large for his mop of black hair, materialized suddenly before me. When I looked down after watching some climbers high on the face of the pyramid, he asked, "Want a genuine antique? Very old!"

A grubby little hand held a hideous, poorly-carved statuette fashioned of coarse lava.

"Ancient idol, señor? Ten pesos."

I shook my head, but he held the "idol" closer, pleading, "Eight? Five? Three? What you give?"

"No," I answered, again shaking my head and wagging my forefinger before his eyes, the final negative. I explained that I was an archaeologist and his idol was only a fake.

He grinned and put it in a ragged coat pocket.

"You are my first customer today. It is bad luck that you do not buy," he said, and then brought out a small green stone from another pocket. I examined it and saw that it had been fashioned, probably with an emery wheel, and buffed, to represent a seated man wrapped in a serape. Some of the features were like those of typical archaeological specimens, but the natural stone had been modified slightly.

The eyes of the little boy never left my face as I handled the carving, a distinctive work of primitive art, created by a real artist.

"You like it?" he asked hopefully.

"It's not old," I said. "Did you make it?"

"For myself," he nodded. "You keep it, señor."

His eyes sparkled when he saw my reciprocal "gift" of a ten-peso note — all of eighty cents. When I praised his work on the little figure, his face beamed:

"I want to be a sculptor, señor. Make things I like — but the *turistas* won't buy."

Now, whenever I look at the little primitive work of art, I think how lucky I was to have been the young sculptor's first customer that day. Otherwise, he might never have parted with it, even as a gift in order to assure his day's luck as a salesman.

But the longer I look at the faint smile on the face of the little stone figure, the more it seems to turn into a sly grin. I'm sure the "gift," which the little sculptor and super-salesman sensed I would prize, was made knowing that I would return one far greater than any amount for which he could ever hope to sell the little figurine.

— Photographed by Helga Teiwes, Arizona State Museum

"Peculiar things" are the stuff of which legends are born — they may come to possess those who create legends. Even clues that have originated as fakes, frauds, or hoaxes, are a part of the answer to the question: What is a legend made of?

The only clue Coronado had to the Seven Cities of Cibola was the copper bell given to Cabeza de Vaca. When this failed to lead to the treasures he was seeking, Coronado created his own legend of Gran Quivira from the hoax provided by The Turk.

Sergeant Jones' clue may have been the spring house with his initials on a nearby tree, carved in reverse as his secret mark.

Rod made pots of gold from pieces of broken pottery that glittered in the bright Mexican sunlight.

And I must have turned some samples of uranium-bearing rocks into a mountain of rich ore.

But without a place in which to look for what the clues demanded, none of the visions that were born of them could have come to any of us.

A CLOUD, A SHADOW, OR A RAINBOW may be an elusive clue that leads to a place where golden fantasies and visions are born.

Visions may be created to fulfill wishful longings. Some of these visions have grown into legends of hidden treasures that are often pursued for the power that only wealth can provide. Visions often furnish nothing more than enjoyment in the search itself, an adventure of looking in strange places and following exotic clues without gaining anything more than an exciting exercise of imagination and of muscles; anything that may be found becomes a treasure — a pot of gold would be fine. For many more, who neither long for legendary wealth nor the search for adventure, legends provide more than riches alone can purchase. To them, legends are folkways, enjoyed by all who care to listen to their telling or to read of them.

Material gains that come from visions of creating wealth may soon be forgotten. But visions which exist only in the minds may last forever if there is a place in which to seek their fulfillment. Legends never die!

References and Notes

MOST OF THE LEGENDS I heard, sometimes only as snatches of guarded secrets told by a cautious treasure seeker, have since been published in folklore journals, magazines, newspapers, and numerous books. There are many versions of each. Some accounts are related as actual records of treasure. Others are simply tales of the searches that have been made for legendary wealth.

For those who may want to know more of the legends themselves than my encounters with them, a comprehensive list of Southwestern publications is to be found in the late J. Frank Dobie's *Guide to Life and Literature of the Southwest,* published by Southern Methodist University, Dallas, 1952; also, in Richard S. Ladd, *A Descriptive List of Treasure Maps and Charts in the Library of Congress,* Library of Congress, Washington, 1964.

National magazines, such as *Argosy* and *True,* and daily newspapers frequently carry stories of hidden treasures. For example, the subject has been featured by *Desert Magazine* and is often included in other Southwestern publications.

Legends of lost mines often originated in the Mexican and earlier periods such as is recorded in the *Rudo Ensayo* (Rough Essays) by an unknown Jesuit priest, first published by Buckingham Smith in 1863, translated by Eusebio Guitéras and published in English, Vol. V, No. 2, *Records of the American Catholic Historical Society,* Philadelphia, 1894; and republished by *Arizona Silhouettes,* Tucson, 1951.

The legends are frequently kept alive by later eye-witness accounts as recorded in *Adventures in the Apache Country* by J. Ross Browne, first published by Harper & Brothers, New York, 1869, and reprinted by *Arizona Silhouettes,* Tucson, 1950.

The Mormon story has been told in many ways since the publication of the *Book of Mormon* in 1830: official histories are those by Joseph Smith, *History of the Church of Jesus Christ of Latter-day Saints,* Period I, 3 Vols., Deseret Book Co., Salt Lake City, 1951, 2nd edition revised; and by B. H. Roberts, *A Comprehensive History of the Church of Jesus Christ of Latter-day Saints,* 6 Vols. and Index, Brigham Young University Library (1931), 1959. Publications with other viewpoints are not uncommon as recorded in *Saints of Sage and Saddle: Folklore Among the Mormons* by Austin and Alta Fife, Indiana University Press, Bloomington, 1956; and *Origin of the Book of Mormon,* by Perry Benjamin

Pierce, *American Anthropologist,* (N.S.) pp. 674–694, G. P. Putnam Sons, New York, 1899.

Interest in elephants in America started early and soon grew into widespread controversy as shown by numerous publications such as: *Elephants and Ethnologists,* by G. Elliot Smith, E. P. Dutton and Co., New York, 1924.

NOTES

[1] Frank Dobie, *Apache Gold and Yaqui Silver* (Boston: Little, Brown and Co., 1939), pp. 185–259.

[2] Eldred D. Wilson, "Early Mining in Arizona," *The Kiva,* (Tucson: Arizona State Museum, May 1946), XI, No. 4, 39–47.

[3] Roscoe P. Conkling, *The Butterfield [Trail] Overland Mail Route, 1857–1869* (Glendale, California: The Arthur H. Clark Co., 1947), Map, Vols. I, II, III.

[4] Rufus Kay Wyllys, *Arizona, The History of a Frontier State* (Phoenix: Hobson & Herr, 1950).

[5] George P. Hammond and Agapito Rey, *Narratives of the Coronado Expedition 1540–1542* (Albuquerque, New Mexico: University of New Mexico Press, 1940), p. 197.

[6] Frederick W. Hodge (ed.), "The Narrative of Alvar Núñez Cabeza de Vaca," in *Spanish Explorers in the Southern United States* (New York: Barnes & Noble, Inc., 1907), pp. 1–26.

[7] Hammond and Rey, p. 42.

[8] Hammond and Rey, p. 43.

[9] Edwin Place (ed. and ann.), *Amadís de Gaula* (Madrid, 1962); original published in Zaragoza, Spain, 1508.

[10] Hammond and Rey, pp. 65–66.

[11] Hammond and Rey, pp. 1–33.

[12] Hammond and Rey, p. 177.

[13] Hammond and Rey, pp. 278–279.

[14] George Parker Winship, "The Coronado Expedition 1540–1542," *14th Annual Report,* U.S. Bureau of Ethnology, 1892–3 (Washington, D.C., 1896), p. 472.

[15] Harold Bell Wright, *The Mine with the Iron Door* (New York: Appleton, 1923).

[16] Charles W. Polzer, S. J., "Jesuit Gold," *The Desert Magazine,* (Palm Desert, Calif.), XXV, No. 8, (August, 1962), 22–27.

[17] Dobie, pp. 3–124.

[18] *Arizona Daily Star,* [Tucson], Nov. 12, 1959.

[19] Anita Brenner, *The Wind that Swept Mexico* (New York: Harper & Bros., 1943). (The history of the revolution, 1910–1942, with 184 historical photographs assembled by George R. Leighton).

[20] James Atwater, "Spanish Gold Two Fathoms Deep," *The Saturday Evening Post,* No. 44 (Dec. 12, 1964), pp. 66–71.

[21] Rachel French, "Alamos — Sonora's City of Silver," *The Smoke Signal, The Westerners,* (Tucson, 1962), No. 5.

[22] *Geological Survey of Texas,* 2nd Annual Report (Austin, 1890), pp. 449–55.

23 Randolph B. Marcy, *Exploration of the Red River of Louisiana* (Washington, D.C.: Robert Armstrong Public Printer, 1853).

24 Steve Wilson, "Strange Maps to the Spider Rock Treasure," *Argosy* (Popular Publications, Inc., New York), CCCLX, No. 5, May, 1965, 40–43, 114–18.

25 James Churchward, *The Lost Continent of Mu* (New York: Ives Washburn, 1931), pp. 17–21.

26 James Churchward, *The Children of Mu* (New York: Ives Washburn, 1945), pp. 290–92.

27 Roscoe Willson, "Arizona Rock Pictures Need a Rosetta Stone," *Arizona Days and Ways [Sunday] Magazine,* (Phoenix: Arizona Republic, January 31, 1965), pp. 26–27.

28 William Edwin Berrett, *The Restored Church, A Brief History of the Growth and Doctrines of the Church of Jesus Christ of Latter-day Saints* (4th ed.; Department of Extension of the Church of Jesus Christ of Latter-day Saints, 1944; distributed by the Deseret Book Company, Salt Lake City), pp. 62–5.

29 Joseph Smith, *Joseph Smith Tells His Own Story* (Salt Lake City: Deseret News Press), pp. 1–14.

30 *Ibid.,* p. 4.

31 *Ibid.,* p. 8.

32 Berrett, p. 52.

33 *Encyclopedia Americana,* International Edition (New York: Americana Corporation, 1963), XXIII, 85–6; J. Alden Mason, *The Ancient Civilizations of Peru* (Baltimore, Md.: Penguin Books, Inc., 1957), pp. 131, 202; Hubert Howe Bancroft, "The Native Races" in *The Works of Hubert Howe Bancroft* (San Francisco: A. L. Bancroft & Co., 1883), III, 241–287, 465–472.

34 Constance Irwin, *Fair Gods and Stone Faces* (New York: St. Martin's Press, 1963), pp. 260–61.

35 Berrett, p. 40.

36 Berrett, p. 45.

37 Lord Kingsborough (Edward King), *Antiquities of Mexico* (London: A. Aglio, 1830–48), 9 vols.

38 Francisco López de Gómara, *The Conquest of the West Indies* (New York: Scholars' Facsimiles & Reprints, 1940); original published in 1578.

39 A. P. Maudslay (trans.), Bernal Díaz del Castillo's *The Discovery and Conquest of Mexico, 1517–1521* (Genaro García, Mexico; New York: Farrar, Straus and Cudahy, 1956).

40 Charles Cullen (trans.), Francisco J. Clavijero, S. J., *History of Mexico* (London: Robinson, 1787; printed by W. Prichard, Richmond, Virginia, 1806), 3 vols.

41 Aileen O'Bryan, *The Dîné: Origin Myths of the Navaho Indians,* Bureau of American Ethnology, Bulletin 163 (Washington, D.C.: Smithsonian Institution, 1956), p. 16, fig. 1.

42 Vernon C. Allison, *The Antiquity of the Deposits in Jacob's Cavern,* Anthropological Papers of the American Museum of Natural History (New York, 1926), XIX, Pt. 6, 291–335.

43 Ronald L. Ives, "The Monster of Quitovac," *The Masterkey* (Los Angeles: Southwest Museum, 1941), XV, 195–99.

44 Frederick Bennett Wright, *Records of the Past,* (Washington: Records of the Past Exploration Society, 1903), II, Pt. 8, 253; Vol. II, Pt. 9, 288.

45 G. Elliot Smith, *Elephants and Ethnologists* (New York: E. P. Dutton & Co., 1924).

46 Churchward, 1945, p. 34.

47 Berrett, p. 45.

[48] John Ranking, *Historical Researches on the Conquest of Peru, Mexico, Bogotá, Natchez and Talomeco in the 13th Century By Mongols Accompanied with Elephants* (London: Longman, Rees, Orme, Brown and Green, 1827).

[49] J. Frank Dobie, *Coronado's Children* (New York: Grosset & Dunlap, 1930), pp. 335–37.

[50] Dorothy Smith Sides, *Decorative Art of the Southwestern Indians* (New York: Dover Publications, Inc., 1961).

[51] LeRoy H. Appleton, *Indian Art of the Americas* (New York: Charles Scribner's Sons, 1950).

[52] David Diringer, *Writing* (New York: Frederick A. Praeger, 1962), p. 176; Fig. 52.

[53] Arizona Livestock Sanitary Board, *Brand Book and Supplement* (Phoenix: State of Arizona, 1953).

[54] Hubert Howe Bancroft, "History of Arizona and New Mexico," in *The Works of Hubert Howe Bancroft* (San Francisco: The History Company, 1889), XVII, 260–62.

[55] F. V. Hayden, *U.S. Geological and Geographical Survey of the Territories for 1874,* 8th Annual Report (Washington, D.C., 1876).

[56] W. H. Holmes, *Report on the Ancient Ruins of Southwest Colorado, 1875–1876,* U.S. Geographical and Geological Survey of the Territories, 10th Annual Report (Washington, D.C., 1878), pp. 3–21.

[57] Frank McNitt, *Richard Wetherill: Anasazi* (Albuquerque, New Mexico: University of New Mexico Press, 1957), pp. 11–22.

[58] *Ibid.,* pp. 38–43.

[59] D. Lloyd Morgan (trans.), Gustaf Erik Adolf Nordenskjöld *Cliff Dwellers of the Mesa Verde* (Stockholm: P. A. Norstedt and Soner, 1893), (New York: Stechert, 1901).

[60] F. W. Putnam, in *Proceedings of the American Association for the Advancement of Science* (Rochester, 1892), p. 297.

[61] Charles Conrad Abbott, *The Stone Age in New Jersey,* Smithsonian Annual Report for 1875 (Washington, D.C., 1875), pp. 246–380.

[62] H. M. Wormington, *Ancient Man in North America* (Denver: Denver Museum of Natural History, 1957), Popular Series No. 4, 4th edition, revised 1957.

[63] Curtis D. MacDougall, *Hoaxes* (New York: Dover Publications, Inc., 1958), pp. 100-102.

[64] Jesse Walter Fewkes, *Archaeological Expedition to Arizona in 1895* (Washington, 1898), USBAE 17, pp .519–752.

[65] Frank Hamilton Cushing, J. Walter Fewkes, and Elsie Clews Parsons, "Contributions to Hopi History," *American Anthropologist,* XXIV, 253–98; Frank Hamilton Cushing, "Outline of Zuni Creation Myths," USBAE, V. 13, Annual Report for 1891–92, pp. 321–447.

[66] Sherman S. Howe, *My Story of the Aztec Ruins* (Farmington, New Mexico: The Basin Spokesman, 1955).

[67] John L. Stephens, *Incidents of Travel in Central America, Chiapas and Yucatan* (New York: Harper & Bros., 1841), Vols. I and II.

[68] Brigham Young University, *Papers of the Fourteenth Annual Symposium on the Archaeology of the Scriptures,* University Archaeological Society, Provo, Utah, 1963.

[69] Welby W. Ricks, "A Purported Phoenician Inscription in New Mexico," *Papers of the Fifteenth Annual Symposium on the Archaeology of the Scriptures,* (Provo, Utah: Brigham Young University, May 16, 1964), pp. 94–100.

Index

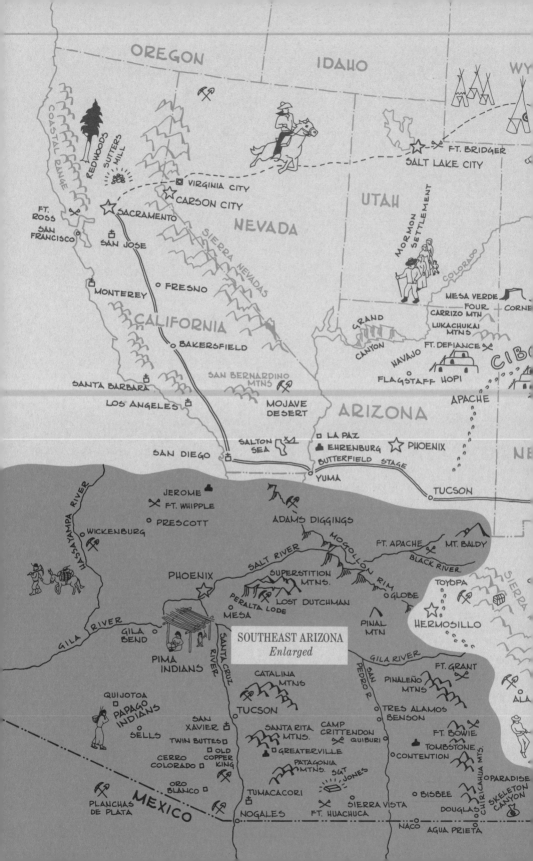